The Art of JAPANESE GARDENS

Designing & Making Your Own Peaceful Space

HERB GUSTAFSON

David & Charles

Book design by Judy Morgan
Edited by Rodman Neumann

A DAVID & CHARLES BOOK

First published in the UK in 1999 by David & Charles
Brunel House, Newton Abbot, Devon
First published in the USA by Sterling Publishing Company, Inc.
387 Park Avenue South, New York, N.Y. 10016

A catalogue record for this book is available from the British Library.

ISBN 0 7153 0986 2

Printed in China

Acknowledgments

I would like to recognize and pay respect to the many professors, teachers, and fellow apprentices who worked with me in Japan and China. Without that powerful personal experience and their generously shared knowledge, this work would not have been possible.

The practical experience I have since gained from countless Japanese garden projects, large and small, with which I have been fortunate to be involved humbles me greatly. I thank all of my sponsors for their support as I grew along with their gardens.

Thanks go to Bob Baltzer for allowing me to photograph some of his many Japanese maples in the fall color that adorn these pages.

Joyce Temby has provided me with accurate photographic record-keeping, document retrieval, and word processing of this manuscript. Her ever faithful organizational skills and gentle prodding helped me with the task, in spite of numerous technical and personal disasters.

As always, I thank my father for his unjudgmental love and support. Thank you, Annie-dog, for your constant and dependable affection.

Herb L. Gustafson

CONTENTS

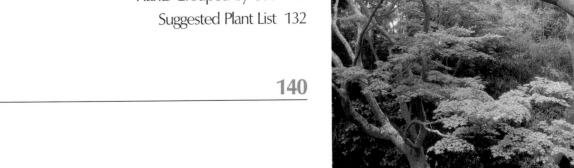

PREFACE

We have made it this far.
Do we want to turn back?
Do we wish to continue
the same path or change
direction? We pause a
moment to reflect on our
journey thus far.
Then we move on.

The Japanese garden means many things to us. For some, it is the place we go to view ponds, curved bridges, and artistically placed plants. For others, it offers an escape to Eden, a place of purity and contemplation. Still others might argue that the garden gathers up life's symbolism and displays it back to us as we stroll along the garden's paths.

I would like to make the Japanese garden accessible to all, to offer the repose and satisfaction to anyone who has a space in their world that they would like to make their own. The term "Japanese garden" is an attempt to combine many facets and approaches to garden space that are enjoyed in Japan. Some garden design originated thousands of years ago outside the borders of Japan—indeed, even before Japan existed as any sort of unifed nation. This book makes no attempt to be a complete study of Zen philosophy, nor does it try to trace the enormous history and contributions to garden design that we have gleaned from the Japanese. It is my wish, rather, to offer an inspiring, yet practical, work that will bring the Japanese garden into your home landscape. You will discover the great diversity of plant material available in North America suitable for your project. You will also be pleased to discover that among the many styles of Japanese gardens, there is one that suits your growing space and personal style.

The traditional Japanese garden brings to the viewer a vast array of symbolic representations. It is my wish to bring this information to the garden in a nonthreatening manner. The Japanese *niwa* is special because of its double meaning as both "garden" and "place." It is not merely an artistic arrangement of rocks, trees, and water. The very shape of these elements cries out for recognition on a higher plane. We see the combining of the primitive earthly elements: the air above and the water below. The earth is represented by the skeletal structure of stones protected by the integument of topsoil. Our origin in fire is seen as beacons to our future placed in the stone lanterns to guide us among the *rati*, or path. Our gardens can become a profound representation of the universe as a whole.

With the knowledge we gain about the combining of these garden elements, we raise our enjoyment level. Our personal experience of the Japanese garden is a product of our efforts to understand its many levels of meaning. If we strive for a heightened awareness of the interplay of its components, we take back greater satisfaction. The Eden of niwa exists mainly in our imagination. Universal spirit is the tool that the visitor uses to glean the fullest satisfaction out of the experience. Plus, the fulfillment of creating with our own hands a personal garden of our own design adds to the enjoyment. The more you can put into the experience in terms of labor and knowledge, the more the garden will return to you in personal satisfaction.

chapter 1

BOUNDARIES

One expects that this special walk leads to an important teahouse or overlook. Perhaps a large pond awaits us just around the corner.

FENCES

Their Function

Of all the boundaries we see in the Japanese garden, fences are the most common. They are familiar to us because we live in a world that depends, for many reasons, on fences. Fences outside the garden environment serve many functions that are useful within the garden as well. They give us privacy and security, delineate boundaries, provide backgrounds and backdrops. Fences let us know where it is appropriate to go in a garden setting. The Japanese garden is a place we go to for comfort. The paths we take and the views we observe are often guided by fences. The notion that we are being excluded from an area by a fence is minimized by using construction materials and designs that are natural and unobtrusive. We see the use of unstained wood and bamboo. Fences become borders more than privacy or security structures. They form the framework for the garden area, as well as guide our footsteps through the unguided tour we have come to associate with this art form.

Cedar

A rather classic style of fence made entirely of cedar is shown in **1-1**. Square 4 x 4 inch cedar posts four feet long are placed closely together in the ground. Notches are made on two sides of the posts to accommodate the horizontal 1 x 2 inch cedar strips. The notches can easily be cut with a one-inch-wide wood chisel and mallet. Only two horizontal strips are needed to demarcate the two sides of this fence. There is enough flexibility in the posts to allow the insertion of the strips into the notches. A more difficult construction but stronger fence is made by notching all the way through the posts.

As with all aspects of construction in the Japanese garden, the detail and craftsmanship put into the work provides an important visual effect. Whereever possible, hide screws, nuts, and bolts. I realize that hardware is often necessary for stability, but its evidence detracts from the natural feeling and harmony of the garden.

Acer palmatum 'Samidare,' **Japanese maple**

Acer palmatum 'Sanguineum,' Japanese maple

1-1

Bambusa, bamboo

Use concrete to support your posts. Often a stronger structure can be made by using right-angle bends in an otherwise straight fence. This not only makes the fence resistant to wind, but it visually breaks up the monotony of a straight line. Concrete can be covered slightly with a subtle layer of gravel or sand, in order to maintain the soundness of your support posts and yet satisfy the eye that does not want to see a mound of aggregate at the base of a post.

Bamboo

A remarkably simple bamboo fence that is rich in texture and hue is shown in **1-2**. The posts are clusters of strong vertical bamboo sticks. This example uses only four. For a visually imposing post, variations may utilize dozens of sticks lashed together with raffia. The horizontal members are merely stacked above a predetermined starting point about 16 inches from the ground. Start this fence lower if you need to keep pets out and increase privacy. The lowest level of bamboo should be perfectly level or follow the contours of the ground. Use a tight string to achieve an accurate reference point. The remainder of the construction is easy. Just stack the horizontal bamboo canes until the tops of the posts are nearly reached. Allow enough room to lash the tops of the posts together. For longer fences, trim the

canes so that the joints are hidden inside the posts. For shorter fences or for quick turns in the garden, cut off all the canes to the same length. This fence has a nice decorative bit of black wool yarn used as a tie instead of raffia. Other types of decorative ties are red ribbon, copper wire, and white wool. Arrange a subtle repeating pattern for best results. As with all wood that stays outside, a bit of protective oil such as linseed will keep cracking to a minimum. As soon as you see a great difference in color between wet and dry, it is time to recoat your fence.

A rather crude, yet effective, bamboo fence is shown in **1-3**. The slippery bank between this tree and the stream below was an easy target for excess erosion because of foot traffic and winter rainfall.

This simple structure guides the garden stroller to a safer path from which to view the stream.

1-3

The horizontal bamboo canes have been split with a saw and lashed together, front to back, with black wool yarn. The vertical canes are stacked together at random for a grove effect. The half-cane top serves to finish off the upper frame of the fence and helps keep rainwater out of the hollow upper segments of the vertical canes.

Protect the bottoms of these fences with a bit of household bleach to remove algae, and then finish with a bit of oil for a lasting coating.

Acer palmatum 'Ao shime no uchi,' Japanese maple

Acer palmatum 'Sekimori,' Japanese maple

1-4

minimize rot and decay. The fence also functions visually as a framework around this teahouse. Imagine approaching the building from the garden. Its stark walls are softened by the horizontal railing around it. The Western eye often allows bare walls such as this to be softened with foundation plantings. This only encourages the use of one-sided plantings and draws the eye into gazing at a wall.

The Japanese garden uses a wall or a fence as a starting point rather than a finishing point. The viewer is encouraged by garden design to have his or her back against such rigid devices. The eyes are therefore drawn out into the landscape.

Fence Railing

The cedar fence (*see* **1-4**) serves several purposes. Even though this deck is low enough to be exited on all sides, it guides the visitor to a path in order to protect the ground cover: a dwarf bamboo. This fence provides a secure handrail for gazing out at the garden. Its height also provides support for people to lean against or sit on while conversing. The natural weathered cedar is occasionally treated with oil to

Lath

Thin strips of cedar lath make up the wonderfully simple yet visually complex fence shown in **1-5**.

Acer palmatum 'Viridis,' Japanese maple

Acer palmatum 'Sherwood flame,' Japanese maple

This fence is ideal for areas that are flat, yet the garden curves around a corner. The lacy effect of the sun coming through the lattice is unobtrusive and adds a nice texture and feel to a potentially dark location. Sufficient privacy is attained by keeping the slats about three-quarters of an inch apart. Larger spaces allow more freedom of view and for the escape of light and wind. Slats that are closer together lose the fabric-like quality of this fence. It looks woven, but is not.

Set up your posts at six-foot intervals, curving them with the contour of the garden edge or border. Pre-form the six-foot-square panels at another location, and insert them between the posts after construction. Round six-inch creosote-treated fir posts are good substitutes if cedar, redwood, or juniper posts are unavailable. If the fence must look nice from both sides, merely install a bit of support molding to the posts prior to installation of the slat panels. If the fence is one-sided, the horizontal slats are just nailed or lashed to the back of the posts.

Fabrication of the panels is relatively easy. Locate a flat working surface at least eight feet square. A concrete driveway works well. Putting several worktables togeth-

Acer palmatum 'Koto Moito,' **Japanese maple**

er will also suffice. Measure and lay out the strips precisely with very light pencil marks. Do not try to assemble the whole structure at once. Work from one side

to the other, one lath strip at a time, fastening as you go. For best results, a few drops of exterior wood glue at each joint will make the panel much more rigid than nails alone. Where two wood strips cross each other, the use of a staple is recommended rather than a single nail. The two prongs of the staple add stability to the joint as well as function to clamp the glue.

Border Fence

The fence shown in **1-6** functions more as a visual border than most other similar structures. One can easily imagine this garden path without a fence at all. Where one is supposed to walk is obvious, yet you have to appreciate the construction, the materials, and the design of this fence. The curves of the path are outlined and exaggerated. The fence offers a certain warmth and security to the outdoor setting. Certainly in a public garden this border would offer a hint that walking in the shrubbery is frowned upon. In a private garden, though, a fence of this design is a nice added detail. Its Oriental feel imparts importance to this path. One expects that this special walk leads to an important teahouse or overlook. Perhaps a large pond awaits us just around the corner. I have seen simple border fences like this that add importance to a large wayside planting of Japanese iris. Construction of this type of fence is easy. Pre-drill your posts with a saw made for cutting doorknob holes (it's sometimes called a circle cutter). These special blades are made in many sizes. Have several sizes on hand to match the diameters of the horizontal posts you are using. If a large rail member will not go into your largest hole, just taper it off at the end a bit with a small hatchet or spokeshave. Install your posts as you add the rails. Do not cement in all your posts first: You will not be able to insert your rails later.

1-7

Safety Rail

A decorative variation on the previous border-type fence is shown in **1-7**. The round posts have been run through a lathe to decorate their tops. A crude notch toward the top of a post can also be added with an axe-cut or chisel. A subtle design can be applied with paint. Imagine these same posts with two black stripes around the tops where the lathe cuts are now located. The effect would be similar.

Since this fence functions as a safety rail and handhold, make sure that it has at least two rungs or horizontal rails. This will add strength as well as provide additional protection for children.

Note the narrow size of the rails. They are strong enough to support an unsteady hand, yet do not block the view of the distant waterfall tumbling into this stream. Special construction of fences for safety are necessary around water, even in a private garden. If you have any doubts about the necessity of safety railings in your garden, consult your local building or construction codes.

Fences do not have to merely include or exclude people. They can decorate our yards and change the direction of our footsteps. Lattice can partially mask an interesting view and illuminate it with the sun at the same time.

Lattice can be formal, rustic, or contemporary. Its textures can come from a wide variety of building materials. Before the construction of a garden fence, visualize in your mind all the nuances of color, texture, size, and style. Fence selection is not a portion of garden design to be trifled with. It is as important as plant selection and path direction. It often is the framework and background for the garden itself. The fences are backbones of style and position. They determine where the view starts and ends, and in the largest sense this element of perception and viewpoint is the embodiment of the Japanese garden.

WALLS

Various Uses

When we compare the appearance and function of walls with those of fences, a few profound differences emerge. Walls tend to be formidable structures. They are often thicker, higher, and heavier. But just like fences, they can serve many functions, even simultaneously. A stone wall can exclude visitors from a garden area as well as buttress a slope to control erosion. Some walls can be interior to the garden, such as surrounding a shrine, yet serve to guide the stroller on the outside. Walls can contain, protect, hide, or limit access. Like fences, they sometimes provide a backdrop when the distant view would normally be too cluttered.

Retaining Walls

A stone structure that functions nicely as a retaining wall is shown **1-8**. The natural stone surface is pleasant in appearance and is expertly crafted. A construction of this magnitude in a private garden is contracted through construction companies that specialize in stone masonry. Unless you are young, strong, and very experienced in the placement of stone, I would recommend hiring out projects such as this to a licensed contractor.

Notice that the wall is not vertical; it slopes slightly toward the earth mass behind it. This angle functions structurally to offset the push of the earth mass behind, as well as functions to relax the eye. Consider this wall as absolutely vertical. As you stroll past this retaining wall, you would question its stability. As an owner, you might even be inclined to get your level and check to see if it had moved after last winter's

1-8

1-9

storms. The visual calm we receive from slightly angled walls like this is subtle, for sure. But a vertical retaining wall is noticeable indeed; we immediately experience a sense of instability from the aesthetic imbalance.

Notice also the "weep holes" provided by the builder in the bottom third of this view. These holes are spaced along the bottom of the entire length of the wall to prevent it from retaining water. If the earth mass behind this structure were to be too tightly contained, the plants up above would be growing in a soggy soil and would not thrive. Also, by allowing excess water to weep through these holes, the weight of the earth mass stays fairly constant and there is reduced danger of water-induced erosion on the slope.

Privacy

The wall shown in **1-9** is fairly plain. It provides little security; a motivated intruder could grasp the tiles at the top and throw a leg over its five-foot peak without much trouble. This particular wall is designed for meditation in a seated position on one of the benches provided. The wall actually encloses a raked sand-and-stone garden. Its color and texture serve to exclude the clutter around the immediate area.

Prunus sargentii 'Columnaris,' **Japanese sargent cherry**

1-10

Salix Babylonica, weeping willow

One cannot be seen from the outside while seated. The sun and rain, moon and stars are admitted to this space, but not the distraction of twiggy branches and fallen leaves. There is privacy both in and out. The mind is free to internalize. Our sights and sounds are reduced, thereby allowing the imagination within to predominate. It is a bit like closing your eyes while keeping them open. This used to be a favorite place for me to go after a particularly grueling mid-term exam for a difficult course. The lack of input was refreshing by comparison to the demands made on me only a few hours before.

Structures

It may not be immediately evident, but when we come across a structure such as the one shown in **1-10**, we actually have two walls. The first wall is the most obvious. It is the wall that includes the bench and the window. The other wall is what we do not see—the exterior wall that gives us the privacy we seek. Structures such as this give us our resting places. We might find them at the top of a long series of steps or midway up a hilly slope. They might function as a rest stop or moon-viewing station. They are most often placed where the view is important.

A peaceful waterfall

A koi pond

Sitting on this bench, we might gaze out at a waterfall or koi pond. There might be an important focus tree artfully framed by a nice bamboo lattice background. This could be the place to relax after a dip in the hot springs. This structure is simply a free-standing wall, one that includes and one that excludes— one that encloses and embraces

while the exterior rejects and reroutes our footsteps.

I came across the bamboo wall shown in **1-11** in Japan. It was made of prunings off the extensive bamboo grove nearby. As the young canes were removed during garden thinning and maintenance, they were cut into standard lengths and stacked on top of this wall. As the older compost

at the bottom of the wall deteriorated, new canes were stacked above to restore the original height.

What a remarkable idea! A totally refreshing application for what might normally be just a compost pile. It was quite a formidable structure as well. I doubt that anyone could climb it without tearing or collapsing sections of it. This is something an intruder abhors.

Some years ago, I visited a bonsai garden in California that was protected by a normal cedar fence topped by a rather flimsy cap made of shingles and lath strips. I commented to the owner about the ease with which an intruder could pull that top structure down and gain entrance to the bonsai area. He laughed at my question and said, "Do you have any idea how much noise that would make? The snapping and popping of all those frail pieces of wood would wake the entire neighborhood!"

1-11

Pinus densiflora, Japanese red pine

As with most structures, there are dangers in trying to categorize them too rigidly. When does a wall become a fence? What keeps a fence from becoming a section of a garden building? And so on. The wall/fence shown in **1-12** is a tall and strong structure of woven bamboo. It functions as a wall and is included in this section. It is thick; you cannot see through it anywhere. It is tall, about seven feet high. The top of the wall is frilly and protective. Its slight overhang provides security as well as a visual endpoint that is pleasing and natural. The visitor is guided to the gate rather convincingly. This is one remarkable facet of the Japanese garden. It is rare that you do not know

where to go. Sometimes you might be given a choice of directions, but they are both correct. Walls do not have to be intimidating. They can guide us on our way, freeing our minds for more pleasant thoughts rather than getting us lost or causing us to stray into an unauthorized area. Sometimes I get a chuckle out of an American park with *Keep Off the Grass* signs all over.

Added Detail

I finished a nice railing for a client and they complained that it didn't look very strong. I jumped up on top of the railing and walked along the top of its length in order to assure them of its

1-12

integrity. Pleased with my balancing act and salesmanship, I inquired whether further work was needed. The client still had an uncomfortable feeling because the railing, while clearly very strong, "looked" weak. I agreed to add additional supports and hardware, not because the railing needed them structurally, but because I understood the concept of visual comfort in a sturdy railing. If a structure looks safe—particularly a railing—it provides visual and structural comfort.

Responding to my client's concerns, I was able to add not only visual stability to the railing but, in doing so, detail. The eye felt comfortable moving from brace to bolt. The regular pattern of wooden pegs and slotted joints made the rail "look Japanese." Before, it was Scandinavian in appearance, with an austere simplicity of design. The added detail made it look stronger and blend with the surrounding garden.

1-13

The brace shown in **1-13** is another example of added detail. Imagine the plain back wall of this structure without the bamboo focus. The structure would look like the back of a storage shed, uninteresting and uninspired. The bamboo highlight visually supports the wall, breaks up the flat monotony, provides framework for the heavenly green bamboo, *Nandina domestica*, and adds a nice touch of detail to the scene. Look for places in your garden to introduce a nicely detailed birdhouse, weather vane, or sculpture. Such details are important.

Acer palmatum 'Omato,' Japanese maple

Acer macrophyllum, large-leaf maple

The carving along the wall seen in **1-14** is elaborate and complex, but it changes a plain structure into a focal point with visual impact. Obviously, these details were created by a skilled woodcarver. For others, who might be less inclined to tackle such an extensive project, consult your local home improvement center. I have seen wonderful precarved or molded filigrees that can be added to gates or ornamental structures. Some of these products are of cast or formed plastic that looks like wood and would last quite well in an exterior application, such as to decorate windows and doors. A bit of detail can brighten up a bridge railing or signpost. Choose Oriental patterns for the best results.

GATES

Their Importance

In a typical garden, the gate that allows people to enter is of little significance. It is normally a four-foot-wide hinged structure that resembles the fence that comes up to its edges. A latch allows the garden visitor to open, close, and even lock the garden area at will. It is normally of no importance other than its utility and function. When it is open, the dog gets out. When it is closed, you might be having a barbecue—to which your neighbor was not invited. When it is locked, you are on vacation.

The Japanese garden gate, by contrast, is often one of the most elaborate structures in the garden. Most often, it is covered. A guest may sit on a bench to one side—out of the elements. A traveler to the garden is invited to rest in the shade. Perhaps running water trickling out of a bamboo cane urges the stroller to cleanse his hands and spirit by touching the water to his forehead with a moistened fingertip.

1-14

1-15

The gate shown in **1-15** is, at once, both the end of one journey and the beginning of another. The Japanese revere and respect the passage of time. Passing through a garden gate marks the moment in your life when you leave the cares of the day and enter a peaceful place. The gate is not merely the passage from one space to another, although that is certainly one of its functions. The symbolic importance of a gate can be seen in Western culture: We refer to the "Pearly Gates" or we "open the gates" as we set off into an unknown venture. The Japanese garden is replete with such symbolism. Enjoyment of the garden experience is intensified by our subtle recognition of these deeper meanings. This is one of the joys that can be found in exploring a Japanese garden. Most languages recognize the profound double meanings inferred in such phrases as "we will cross that bridge," "lead us down the garden path," or "pass through that gate when we come to it." These are familiar expressions in the Japanese language as well. They heighten our living experience and make our passages through the gates of time important.

Nandina domestica,
heavenly bamboo

The Garden Entrance

A simple gate, such as the one in **1-16**, can mark the boundary of the garden and look inviting as well. With one door closed and one door open, we are reminded of the expression "One door doesn't close that does not open another." We seek shelter from the rain at such an important crossroad, or respite from the heat of the day. The garden is not visible from the gate, but the path is evident. Notice that the stone path has changed in appearance somewhat. It is still a path, but its slightly different construction infers that the path will be obvious—just a bit different. The bulk of the garden is only around the corner. We are invited to pause and reflect before taking that first step on a slightly different path to see what is around the next corner.

The Tile Roof

I am sure we all have seen the incredible tile roofs found on important structures in Japan. The reader is presumed to have more than just a passing interest in the Japanese garden if he has perused this book this far. Even if you have not been to Japan, North American Japanese gardens display many temples, pavilions, and teahouses with this type of roof (*see* **1-17**). They are certainly grand and glorious to behold. Japanese import companies can provide you with these tiles. But for the most part, we do not see such elaborate work in smaller private gardens. I built a teahouse for a client that used cedar shingle in much the same pattern, and it turned out quite nice. With some flexibility and a great deal of imagination, you can construct roof details of which you are proud. A local roofing contractor

1-16

1-17

may have some ideas to help you achieve precisely the look you want within your budget. This particular tile roof is above a grand gate.

A Simple Gate

The detail of a practical gate is shown in **1-18**; the gate is easily constructed with Western materials. A 6 x 6 inch vertical cedar post supports a shingle roof overhead. A horizontal 2 x 8 inch fir beam is locked into position with a simple wedge. The adjoining gate has a wrought-iron hinge and the door is functionally decorated with wooden pegs.

1-18

1-19

The Entrance Planting

Entrances and exits to and from the garden are often decorated with cut flowers or a vase with a decorative planting in it. Sometimes a large bonsai is placed on a stone stand, such as that shown in **1-19**, to greet the guest. Tradition has it that you compliment your guest with the importance of the planting; ikebana for the lady, and a fine old pine tree for the gentleman. Note the construction of the fence in the background. It is elevated on concrete blocks to prevent rot.

1-20

Gate Design Details

The gate shown in **1-20** is another of those grand gates that we wish we had in our garden, but don't. Mainly I want you to look closely at this wonderful gate so you can adapt some ideas for construction of your own gate. The fine lath work under the roof canopy can add textural detail to an otherwise boring soffit. The wooden pegs, large and small, give strength to the design. The windows are present for their effect only; there is no actual interior. Similarly, the balcony railing does not supply security. These are architectural structures that symbolize strength and importance. Incorporate elements such as these freely into your own design. I especially like the colors that the wood is stained. The earth-brown shades make the green pine tree look vibrant in color. A brightly painted gate would detract from the soft green foliage of the garden.

1-21

CONSTRUCTION TECHNIQUE

In the previous section of fences, I showed some simple construction methods. The close-up photograph **1-21** shows a different design that makes a particularly strong gate. It can be used for a fence as well. This gate was made with only a hand chisel and a mallet, but faster and more accurate work can be accomplished with a router and wood joiner tools. The complete absence of hardware, nails, and reinforcement makes this gate wonderful to behold. It is a magnificent example of understatement. Its craftsman must be proud.

chapter 2

ROCKS, BOULDERS & STONES

Look for a story, theme, or parable. It is possible and preferable to add an imaginary "life" to your stones.

A NATURAL PLACE IN THE GARDEN

Rocks form the backbone or primary structure of the Japanese garden. Each boulder, rock, stone, and polished pebble has its natural place in the garden scheme. Heavier, angular boulders are half buried in the highest ground, offering mass and stability to the scene. Smaller boulders and stones act as obstacles in the stream or at turns in the path, thereby giving changes in direction a natural sense and meaning. Still smaller water-tumbled pebbles form the bottoms of ponds and streams, reflecting the natural progression of earthly matter from large to small. Collectively, these rocks make up the skeletal structure of the garden.

For Garden Shape

The rocks offer us form and substance for our world. The thin covering of topsoil, which we see, merely forms the skin over these formative rock "bones." The lay of the land is determined by rocky protrusions versus gullies where water flows. The size and type of rock utilized must be carefully considered for consistency. Smooth stones in a high place are as inappropriate as rough stones in a streambed. The position and type must make visual as well as geologic sense.

Except for certain precise exceptions, such as the sand-and-stone garden, hills and valleys lend themselves to a natural placement and rhythm of plants and stones. On higher ground we find taller, more mature trees among massive boulders projecting up out of the topsoil. When we walk in the woods at higher elevations, this is our natural experience, so in the garden we like to simulate that effect.

For Higher Ground

Interesting garden design will often incorporate a shift in elevation. In **2-1** we see a cluster of boulders holding back a slope of climax trees and small shrubs. Some weeping ground cover has been planted in the rock crevices where the soil is spare. This imposing grouping could guard the path to an elevated teahouse or vista overlooking the flatter garden portions below. Rock groupings such as this make an excellent stream source hidden behind their mass. In practical terms, they are also a great way to hide plumbing at the top of a waterfall. The stones should be arranged in a consistent manner.

If the tops are flat, then they should have no obvious exceptions. If one is slanted, then to suggest a natural geological outcrop, make it part of a slanted rock formation that appears to have been exposed by erosion. Never mix colors of stones; they look contrived. If possible, use boulders of varying size, height, width, and depth. If a stone has the suggestion of a face or posture, arrange the other stones to complement that effect. Avoid facing two stones in a confrontational manner; it may give the viewer an uneasy feeling.

2-1

2-2

For Utility & Beauty

Other rocks have non-skeletal ties to the garden design. They include the stepping-stones and the chair-shaped boulders that are placed not for their geologic accuracy but for human ease and comfort. In addition, some are poetry-engraved with haiku and erected in meditative enclaves. Some rocks stand guard as sentinels by the gate. Still others represent parables—as read through their shape and size relationships to each other. Some rock is crushed as gravel and spread out to form a border for a path or to represent the sea. Some magnificent rocks are displayed on their own merit as sculpture or viewing stones. These rocks may resemble distant mountains, waterfalls, animals, or are simply enjoyed for their special color or texture. Specially shaped natural stones can be utilized as water basins, bonsai stands, or simple lanterns. Carved stones form walls, bridges, and foundations for larger structures such as teahouses, pavilions, and grand gates.

For Streams

A grouping of slightly rounded boulders forms the edge of a small stream to the right, shown in 2-2. A naturally hollowed stone delivers water from the upper stream into the still pool below. A series of smooth, flat stones make up the streambed and smaller, round, fist-sized pebbles are seen in the bottom of the pool.

Notice how the lay of the land is formed by the skeletal rocks. It is unnatural to see water flowing from a single high place. It is much better to have the stream form at the conjunction of two high places. The ferns—as well as the Japanese maple, bamboo, and the evergreen shrub *Skimmia japonica*—complete the appearance of a natural wet glade; and, once in a while a goldfish peeks out from under the floating water lilies.

For best results on constructing waterfalls, contain the stream completely with concrete or other impermeable material. Then, while the water pump is operating, move the main stones around with a crowbar until the right water flow and sound are achieved. Turn off the pump, then secure your stones with more hidden cement.

Water sounds best from multiple trickles. Do not focus the stream into a single spill or it will just sound like someone left the faucet running, or worse. Do not worry about growing moss or lichens. They will grow in the appropriate places in time. Often efforts to plug moss into crevices result in an unnatural appearance. If you have bare, new boulders that could use a little "aging," try a few light spritzes of buttermilk to get the mosses started.

Often it is simply a matter of correcting the stones' natural high mineral pH. Vinegar does a nice job of helping exposed concrete to age and darken. I always use a dark dye in my concrete to avoid the new whitewashed appearance after setting.

Bridges & Walkways

An incredible grouping of stones is shown in **2-3** spanning a slow-moving pond. Mosses grow where the friction of footsteps is absent. The narrow cracks between the stones allow for the movement of water, an unusual bridge. The shadows of the stones make them look twice as

Acer japonicum 'Aconitifolium,' **full-moon maple**

2-3

2-4

thick, and koi enjoy swimming the many channels. Construction of this sort of path is fairly easy if the pond can be drained temporarily or if the rocks are set before construction of the stream. Setting the flat tops then becomes no more difficult than leveling the top stonewall or setting large stepping-stones into concrete. Once the pond is filled with water, this type of bridge becomes impractical to build.

Simple Isolated Groupings

The small grassy knoll shown in **2-4** would be rather uninteresting without the grouping of stones. Successful groupings are rather easy to assemble if you lend importance to some simple conventions:

⁕ Use an odd number of rocks. The Japanese have learned that it is easier to arrange clusters of three, five, or seven stones in a natural way. Even numbers have a tendency to appear symmetrical or contrived.

⁕ Vary the sizes of the boulders. If the three rocks in **2-4** were the same size and shape, it would be difficult to make them appear natural.

⁕ Look for a story, theme, or parable. It is possible and preferable to add an imaginary "life" to your stones. With some stretch of the imagination, in example

2-4 one might visualize the boulders as a large, patriarchal elephant seal cradling one of his harem cows while gazing out to sea, the sea represented by the flat rock. The story itself is not as important as the vision. I find that boulders that satisfy an organic relationship look comfortable together.

⁕ Find some common bond in all your stones. Use similar angles in all. Eliminate odd or striking colors and textures. Bury the stones to the same degree and proportion. Line up similar geologic features such as striations, bedding, and weathering detail. The eye picks up these similarities easily as making sense.

Geologic Accuracy

A natural grouping of stones is seen in **2-5**, lining the edge of a lowland to the right. These stones have been placed to border the contour of the land below. They appear as though they remain here due to a lack of stream ero-sion. Indeed, the types of stone utilized have been selected because of their lack of water-induced erosion.

A gathering of smooth stones at this location would appear out of place, and it would be difficult to arrange them to look natural. Notice in particular how the sharp angles are nestled tightly together for protection. This is a fine example of a fabricated geo-logic ridge.

Boulder arrangements should always appear natural, stable, consistent, and timeless. The ridge in **2-5** accomplishes all the goals.

2-5

ROCKS AS PATHS

We are familiar with the garden path as a guiding and directional tool. It is quite natural to use flat stones to guide our feet. Perhaps the oldest paths and roads in the world have been constructed in this manner. Use rocks of similar size and shape. Make sure they are level and secure. In the example shown in **2-6** the stones are embedded in concrete to stabilize them on the steep slope. Stepping on a shifting rock in this location would be unsettling indeed.

As with many Japanese garden designs, the elements match to some degree, but still show their individuality. I find that a pathway of perfectly square or round stepping-stones is contrived and out of place in a Japanese garden. Symmetry such as this is more appropriate in the formal English garden.

Note the similarity of the stones in the path shown in **2-6**; at the same time, each is different, however. If you run across two similar stones during construction, simply separate them from each other to make it difficult for the eye to discover them. I find it convenient and precise to arrange these stones on top of a layer of dry concrete mix and sand. I can then move the stones around easily until just the right effect is achieved—even by walking on the path. When I am satisfied, I water them with a hose or sprinkler. By the next morning, the stones are set.

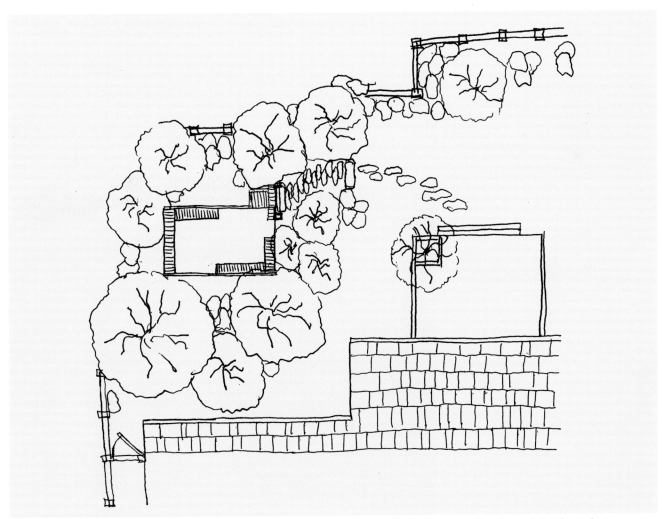

An isolated deck or patio is a nice solution for the smaller or unusually shaped backyard. A stroll along the rock path to the cluster of trees that hides the second patio makes the space seem larger. Privacy is achieved in an area that would normally have none.

2-7

THE SENTINEL STONE

Previously, I suggested attaching importance to your rock groupings by imagining them as animals. The Japanese also use isolated rocks to symbolize warriors, deities, and fictional heroes. The stone in **2-7** is meant to portray the Buddha in a sand-and-stone arrangement. Sentinel stones can represent power, authority, or guardian spirit. They are used at the entrance gate, at important focal points, and wherever their symbolism will enhance the garden experience. To guard the entryway, a convoluted stone might suggest a fierce dragon. A monolith-type vertical boulder can offer blessing and dignity to a teahouse. A human-like form can add compassion and understanding to an otherwise austere flat sand garden. The sentinel stone offers us a suggestion of conscience and higher authority, a guidepost in our personal garden path. Utilize a sentinel stone in your garden with the care, thought, and reverence it deserves.

Acer palmatum 'Dissectum,' Japanese laceleaf maple

2-8

2-9

GRAVEL

Steps

Gravel is, of course, crushed or screened rock, and is therefore included here as one of the sections dealing with rock.

A simple gravel path may be changed into a stairway or even a bridge by forming a series of abutments with wood and filling them in with gravel as shown in **2-8**. Any ground contour can be matched using this simple gravel-fill construction method. The steps can be long or short. They can be made any width. They may curve right or left.

Gravel makes a wonderful, clean material that packs easily and yet drains well. It holds its shape over time, yet can be remodeled easily. This particular example would take just one afternoon to construct, compared to the considerable effort that would be required to duplicate it in timbers, concrete, or boulders. It is a simple, but practical, solution for our garden paths. This gravel-fill technique is very affordable as well as authentic in design.

Paths

Earlier in this chapter, we saw some paths made from rock alone. The type of path shown in **2-9** can be constructed with a base of sand, gravel, mortar, concrete, or a mixture such as exposed aggregate. The flat stones are carefully leveled within a wooden framework that is only meant to be temporary.

Once the design is set, the sand or gravel maintains the rocks in position quite well. For heavy-traffic areas, concrete is best.

2-10

Sand & Stone

In the traditional sand-and-stone garden, as shown in **2-10**, the "sand" is not actually what we Westerners would call sand. It is a crushed light-colored rock, most often granite. We see similar material sold in North America as granite grit. It is somewhat more coarse than the turkey grit that is available at feed stores. Any light-colored finely crushed rock will suffice, such as limestone or quartzite. Look in your local area for a suitable substitute.

The lighter colors represent the sea better than the neutral gray tones found in basalt or other common gravels. The gravel is raked with a coarse wide rake to achieve the effect of "waves" against the isolated rock groupings or islands. Simply walk backwards as you rake, so that you cover up your footprints. With some practice, the raking becomes a pleasant task in the garden. There are many patterns—some curved, wavy, or irregular. Change the pattern often for a varied effect.

Rhododendron 'Coral bells,' *Kurume azalea*

Prunus lusitanica, Portugal laurel

Pieris japonica, **lily-of-the-valley shrub**

Simplicity

How gravel can be used as a combination path and ground cover is shown in **2-11**. The visual effect is quite serene and uncomplicated. The plants are striking in this style, with nothing to detract from their color, form, and texture.

There are no garden borders to construct or maintain, and certainly no lawn to mow!

This use of gravel is best in entryways, courtyards, or atriums. It is a simple but elegant solution to lowering your maintenance in tight or limited-access situations.

2-11

Maintenance & Utility

I found the task of weeding the gravel area in **2-12** daunting. The traditional Japanese method of weeding such an expanse is shown in **2-13**.

I tried to imagine myself squatting down for days on end, cleaning that much area with a small basket and a chopstick! Frankly, I prefer the limited use of short-term herbicides and a long-handled hoe.

By raking your gravel often, you stir up sprouting weed seeds and disturb their development. I recommend a depth of at least six inches. This will discourage wind-blown seeds from finding soil. It is not necessary to lay

2-12

Betula platyphylla 'Japonica,' Japanese white birch

Chamaecyparis obtusa 'Hinoki nana,' dwarf hinoki cypress

2-13

down black plastic sheeting under the gravel. This only blocks proper drainage and spoils the soil. One of the joys of a gravel bed is that it is a rain-water-permeable surface. Unlike surfaces that have to direct water flow, gravel allows the passage of natural rain into the groundwater system. In many areas, concrete requires a building permit where-as gravel does not.

chapter 3

WATER

The stream is the natural movement of fluid through the garden, its source and destination out of sight. Our footsteps follow along its banks. We sit and are relaxed by the never-ending flow.

THINGS TO CONSIDER

If rocks form the skeletal structure of the garden and the contour of the topsoil represents the integument, then water supplies the lifeblood (*see* **3-1**). It can lie still in a pond teeming with lilies and koi or trickle along the low passageways of streams lined with eroded boulders. It can roar at us with the might of a huge waterfall or sing us to sleep with a trickled lullaby. Water represents purity and cleanliness, both of body and spirit. We refresh our physical selves with a drop on the tongue and cleanse our mind with the baptismal gesture of a moistened fingertip on our forehead. Thus purified, we enter the gates of the garden.

PONDS

Selecting a Size

Ponds may be very large or quite small. The size of your pond affects the construction cost, methods, materials, drainage methods, and filtration requirements. Fortunately or unfortunately, there are no hard-and-fast rules for pond construction. A simple pond can be made by burying a premade plastic tub in the ground. It can be periodically cleaned by dumping it out once in a while and refilling it with a hose. This simplest of ponds must necessarily be the smallest of ponds, for obvious reasons. As our ponds become larger, it becomes necessary to employ such devices as drains, filters, pumps, and anti-float valves. Waters that are still are high-maintenance areas in our gardens. I would start very small if I were unsure of the task ahead.

3-1

Water can be "represented" by gravel or sand, and therby lower the maintenance headaches.

Ponds breed mosquitoes and green slime, have a fetid odor, and attract nuisance animals such as raccoons, nutria, rats, and opossums. Goldfish or koi are prone to attack by birds of prey. Neighborhood children cannot resist playing in ponds—a potential tragedy.

Plan your pond with a healthy dose of realism and practicality. A carefully planned pond can provide your garden with as much joy and beauty as you might imagine. If in doubt of your knowledge, skills, or energy, consult with a contractor who specializes in pond construction. You might very well prefer to leave the risk in the hands of a licensed professional.

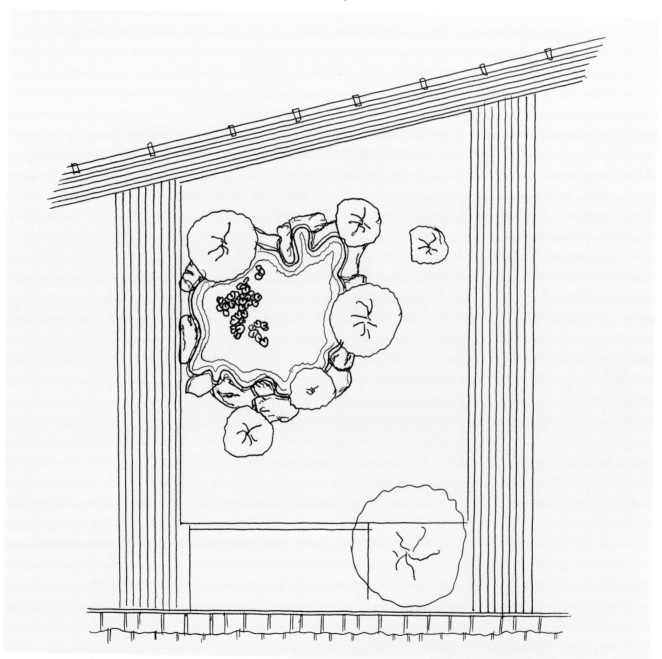

From this small back patio, we can surround a small patio with raised wooden walkways. The water focus is created by hiding the edges of black polyethylene sheets with large rocks. Sprayed Gunnite or poured reinforced concrete may also be used.

Materials

The pond basin itself can be made up of a number of materials. The smallest ponds are plastic tubs molded in irregular shapes and manufactured for use as a sunken container. Larger ponds over eight feet in length can be lined with black polyethylene sheets to slow the leakage of pond water into the ground. If a pond is to be greater than 15 feet across, it becomes desirable to dig the pond in place and spray Gunnite or pour reinforced concrete into its walls to form a permanent basin. Much larger ponds can be created, but they depend on the makeup of the site. The natural presence of a stream allowed me to create a large pond for a customer by using heavy equipment to simply push together a thick earthen dam. The resulting pond surface exceeded half an acre. The project was a huge success. The dam was masked by foliage. The pond outlet to the stream became a nice waterfall with a curved bridge crossing it. Most small pond applications require a pond liner. Large, naturally low areas may be flooded and maintained as a water focus, provided new soils are not brought in that are not tested for stability. Clay is the greatest asset and greatest weakness to large pond construction. It makes a fine pond bottom, but has a nasty habit of moving when used as a supporting side.

Pond Construction

The essential filtration and circulating system components of a garden pond are shown in the schematic drawing below. I will describe each of the various system elements in turn.

The Waterfall

As the pond water is discharged on top of this collection of sand, gravel, pebbles, and stones, it is naturally filtered and aerated just as this happens in a stream. The more length you can construct and the harder the fall, the more benefit you get from this natural biofilter.

The Pond Level

This should be as constant as possible. Visitors to the garden should be able to approach the pond from a safe shelf of concrete-supported stones. In hot weather and in smaller ponds, watch this level daily. Add fresh water to compensate for evaporation and drainage loss (*see* section "The Float" on page 46).

Removable Screen

The screen should have its center at pond level. It should be easily

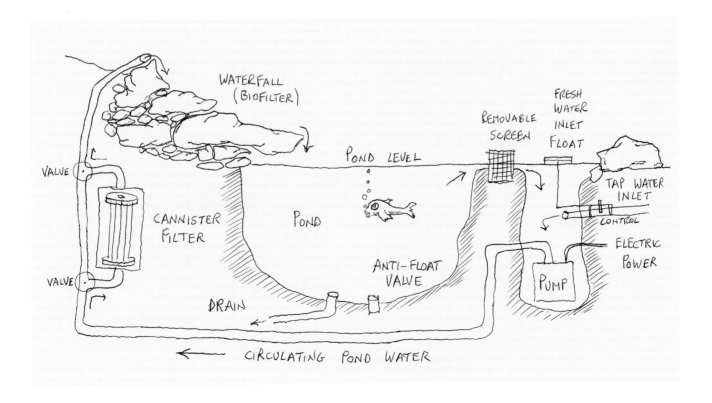

WATERFALL (BIOFILTER)

FRESH WATER INLET FLOAT

REMOVABLE SCREEN

POND LEVEL

VALUE

CANNISTER FILTER

POND

TAP WATER INLET

CONTROL

ELECTRIC POWER

VALUE

ANTI-FLOAT VALVE

DRAIN

PUMP

← CIRCULATING POND WATER

accessible for cleaning and should be removable when this is necessary. I found that common window screen was too fine. Instead, use galvanized or plastic soffit screen ⅛ inch to ¼ inch square. This will eliminate most leaves from entering the submerged pump area.

The Float

Smaller ponds, shallow waters, tall waterfalls, long streams, and hot climates make it desirable to install a float valve on top of your pump well. When the pond level drops, the float detects this drop and triggers a valve that opens the fresh-water inlet. When the surface is restored to its proper level, the float valve closes and stops more fresh water from entering the pond.

The Pump

Many sizes of submersible pump are on the market today. They are rated by GPM or gallons-per-minute output. The GPM rating is often measured at a certain height above the pump level. So, if you have a tall waterfall, be sure to take this into consideration. Submersible pumps are not adjustable. You will have to experiment with several pumps in the right range in order to get the perfect flow over your rocks and waterfall. I personally prefer the slower rates of speed and, therefore, the smaller pumps. A small trickle can be sufficient over time, even from a large waterfall. Remember, you have to live with the sound. To give you

3-2

a frame of reference, compute the GPM from your garden hose, using a timer and a garbage can of known volume. This calculation will give you a rough estimate of how much water flow you desire for your stream; then you can adjust accordingly.

The Anti-Float Valve

This seemingly unimportant device may be the best investment you make in your pond. For only a few dollars you may save yourself a big headache. In areas that have a high water table (most pond locations), you are in danger of floating your pond basin if the pond water level goes down. The most common time for this is during cleaning. You drain the pond and start to scrub the interior surface of slime and algae. All of a sudden the entire pond basin pops out of the ground like a giant cement boat. It tears away the drainpipe, pump pipes, and nice rock edging you have constructed. Oops!

The anti-float valve functions to relieve this pressure from underneath, thereby saving the pond's shell.

The Drain

I realize that it is possible to pump out the pond water, but it is unbelievable how convenient this drainpipe can be during cleaning. It comes highly recommended.

The Cannister Filter

These devices come in many sizes, styles, and purposes. You can make your pond water as clear or as cloudy as you like by adjusting the filter grit size and flow through the cannister. I would highly recommend installing a bypass on your main circulating water line. One gate valve on either side of your cannister will allow you to check your filter at any time while the pump is running. It also allows you to regulate the flow of water through the filter, if necessary.

Pond Banks & Borders

Several varieties of fern can be seen in **3-3**. Ferns are especially effective at the pond's edge, where they are used to visually soften the pond's bank. The natural fluffy fronds of the fern family do a nice job in stabilizing the muddy edge of the pond, as well as present a striking display of foliage that contrasts with the grassy edge and the rocky out-croppings. Ferns enjoy the dampness and the humidity and will reward you with spectacular growth when planted this close to the water.

Water Plants

Always keep in mind that whatever plumbing or filtration devices you utilize, they are kept out of sight. Behind the large clump of iris to the upper right of **3-4**, on page 48, is a fresh-water inlet and float device for maintaining the pond level. It is nicely hidden, yet easily accessible. In the foreground is the popular Japanese iris, and the lotus is blooming nicely right behind it. The iris clumps help prevent bank erosion, and lily pads provide the koi some degree of protection from flying predators. For a complete list of water plants, refer to Chapter Seven.

3-3

Koi

Koi are mouth-breathing carp that can become quite tame (*see* 3-4). You can feed them right out of your hand, though most growers do not recommend touching the fish due to the possible transmission of oils from the hand to their scales. They are long-lived fish and can survive rather large leaps in temperature. They have survived for me under the ice for weeks and seem to do fine in room-temperature shallow water. Provide them with a deep hole in the pond, where they can hide from predators, survive the heat, and rest. Do not allow coins to be dropped into the water, as many do, in order to make a wish. Heavy metals are toxic to fish. A few coins will not have a noticeable effect, but a handful is very unhealthful. Consult with your local koi dealer for specific details about color breeding and health.

Reflecting Pools

One of the nicest attributes to standing water is its ability to reflect what is on land. The Japanese revere this effect and capitalize on it whenever possible. Shape the edge of your pond so that it is irregular, with many fingers of pools branching out in all directions. This will enable you to make the garden path and its resting stations more interesting and integral with the water. We see the reflection of a stone lantern in the water in **3-5**. At night with the lantern lit, we can view a startlingly bright stream of light on the water surface. On a still pond, we would see only two lights: the actual light and a single reflection. As dusk drops, the wind picks up, the fish start to feed, and insects skitter about on the water. The water's ripples turn the reflection into moving ribbons of light that can touch both the near and far shores. Bridges arching over the calm fingers of water become circles, a profound reflection suggestive of the continuity of earth and sky, God and man, and the cycle of life.

3-4

3-6

Viewing Stations

As we travel along the garden path, there are places where the eye wants the legs to stop and rest. At these stations, we provide benches or railings to lean against.

Some of the most spectacular views are bridge overlooks that gaze across a still pond. The view in **3-6** was taken at dawn when the mist still hung heavily over the water, imparting a magical thickness to the liquid. The normally precise construction of water and sky is temporarily clouded, and we can imagine ourselves in some heavenly paradise. The mist moves slowly in the morning breeze until it disappears into the reflections of the sky.

Some time ago, I ran across a university groundskeeper who had neglected to provide any sidewalks that would surely be needed across a great expense of grass. He replied to my inquiry, "In one month I will know where to build the sidewalks." The path becomes where you want to go. The viewing stations are where you want to stop.

WATERFALLS

The Natural Style

There is nothing more peaceful than a walk in the woods on a nice day. Add the sound of water trickling over rocks in a stream and the visual glint of the sun striking a small waterfall in the distance. This scene in **3-7** could be a from a similar experience.

This is not, however, a totally natural mountain trail. It is a portion of a hand-created Japanese garden. We often forget how natural a garden can be. This glade can be created in your own backyard, space willing. Think how refreshing it would be to know you designed and planted it. Sometimes I hear from clients, "The Japanese garden is so contrived." And there are styles that

are. Construct a style that is meaningful to you. Some would say that the scene below is not Japanese at all. Nevertheless, I have hiked the remote woods of Japan and personally experienced it. This natural scenery is universal and has worldwide appeal. It has become known as the natural style, and certainly can be accepted as part of the planned Japanese garden.

For Large, Natural Drops

The waterfall shown in **3-8** is part of a series of falls as an artificial stream makes its way down a steep embankment in a Japanese garden. Obviously, this size fall would be impossible to achieve if your land has little slope. A fall this size could be accomplished on a small lot that had a considerable vertical rise. The boulders are first placed with heavy equipment, then secured with hidden pours of concrete for stability and to contain the water flow. The pumps and filters are hidden with additional stones and foliage, and all you add is time. Natural mosses, algae, lichens, and other ground covers will start to grow if the fall is kept running twenty-four hours a day. Please note that the cost of operating such a pump is quite low. Multiply the power output (found on the pump housing) of your pump by the kilowatt-per-hour electrical rate in your area. In most cases it will not exceed a few dollars per day, even for a fall this size.

Combining Several Falls

A good example of a multitiered waterfall in a Japanese garden is shown in **3-9**. The late winter sun is catching the back sides of the near foliage and leaving the majority of the fall in the distant darkness. Note particularly the similarity of the vertical rock structure among the boulders utilized. Flat tops and vertical sides repeat their patterns in a consistent yet interesting manner. No two rocks are the same size, height, or width, yet the similarity of features provides a consistent design theme that makes the arrangement appear natural. To direct the water in the desired direction, simply alter the height of the stones. Water will naturally flow away from the tallest boulders and settle quite peacefully in the lowest spots.

Notice how the trees and shrubs both soften the flat rock faces and provide a frame for a viewer's eye. At both right and left sides of the stream, low shrubs mask the transition from stone to topsoil—a naturally occurring phenomenon.

3-8

STREAMS

The Water Metaphor

Streams represent the lifeblood of the garden (see **3-10**). They flow from the bottom of the waterfall to the pond. In nature, the conti- nuity of water is the ever-cycling wheel of evaporation, water vapor, condensation, and collection through the intricate streams of the world. In the garden, we artificially pump water from the pond to the top of the waterfall. The water's return to the pond can be slow and lazy or white with froth. Similarly, our bodies pump lifeblood by force into our arteries and veins, where they begin the return trip. Our organs filter the waste for disposal and the cycle begins again. This human analogy adds depth and

3-10

3-11

meaning to the stream. It offers a profound metaphor that we can use in garden design to add to the garden-viewing experience. The stream is the natural movement of fluid through the garden, its source and destination out of sight. We observe only the path and direction of its sustenance, and delight in its murmuring song. We cross its path with bridges that are both simple and complex. Our footsteps follow along its banks. We sit and are relaxed by the never-ending flow.

The Stream Banks

The brightly illuminated stream bank shown in **3-11** is reinforced by stones imbedded in concrete. The artificial edge is masked nicely by plantings of lush ferns and mosses. The dwarf bamboo clumps separate the stream from the building behind.

Access to the stream should be limited to a few select spots in order to protect the integrity of the bank and ensure safety for visitors. Stream sides are always sloped, wet, and slippery. Access to the stream is best accomplished with a series of flat stepping-stones that progress down toward the stream's edge. Positioning these access points on the outsides of stream curves will ensure that the sites are not subject to water erosion, as well as offer the viewer the widest possible waterscape. The example in **3-11** shows how this steep outer curve of the bank can be well protected from erosion and unwanted human entry.

A Simple Stream Crossing

A gently meandering stream tributary ambles across the garden path in **3-12**. These deep stepping-stones comprise one of the simplest ways to cross a stream; we hop from stone to stone just as we used to as a child. This is also very safe.

The railing made of a twisted branch contrasts with the straight sections of railing on either side of the stream. This nicely alerts the visitor to the garden who may wish to gaze at some distant view. The hand touches the railing, which is positioned at a different height than the straight sections, and the twisted texture is immediately felt—thereby alerting the feet to take extra care and caution. The conjunction of these two streams makes a perfect site for a resting rail or a sitting stone. Plant lots of water-loving reeds, thrushes, and bog plants at this convergence. The water here is too shallow for water lilies or lotus, and the koi will be unprotected from waterfowl, so plant the shoreline heavily for best results.

A Large, Meandering Stream

A slow, meandering streambed is shown in **3-13**. Notice the sparse use of stones. The flow of water makes stones unnecessary for this kind of bank reinforcement. The opposite bank is not accessible by foot, so the natural mosses have flourished at the water's edge, providing strong support. Foot traffic in this area would necessitate the construction of a series of flat stepping-stones down to the stream's edge.

This stream is fairly large, deep, and slow-moving, and its pump is fairly small and quiet. This water is not filtered, accounting for its pea-green color.

At dawn the stream is covered by a three-foot-thick layer of mist, making the surrounding trees appear as if they were islands among the clouds. Visualize substituting light-colored gravel for the water. This type of planting would work for locations that do not favor an actual running stream. But dry streambeds are also possible. Just form the hollow of the bed with varying sizes of river rock. Use polished gravel for the deepest "pools." They will appear wet even when they are dry.

3-12

Acer palmatum 'Orangeola,' Japanese maple

Acer palmatum 'Ao shime no uchi,' Japanese maple

A Fast-Moving Rivulet

The slope of the land as shown in **3-14** made it necessary to use a smaller volume of water than you might imagine could flow through the "valley." The sides are well lined with rocks, and the streambed is concrete rather than pebbles or gravel. A pump that is smaller than ones used in previous examples controls the water flow, so erosion does not become a problem. Notice the zigzag motion to the streambed as it falls down the slope. A straight line would appear quite artificial. This small trickle is actually the source of several narrow, but tall, waterfalls along its length. The relatively flat portion serves as an interruption in what would have been only a series of small waterfalls, had the natural slope of the land been utilized. Notice the use of rock walls in the background to stair-step the stream over this moderate slope. The rocky outcroppings on both sides of this gully offer a feeling of stability and longevity to the setting that could not have been accomplished with moss alone.

chapter 4

BUILDINGS
& STRUCTURES

A Chinese-style gazebo in a cultivated Japanese garden is bright and flashy. It bears resemblance to the Victorian garden gazebo with its six sides, high degree of filigree, and views in all directions.

THE PAVILION

The pavilion is historically the largest and most important structure in the Japanese garden. It is a meeting hall, gathering place, shelter, symbol of the garden's grandeur. Visitors to Japan are familiar with the elaborate golden pavilions and other similar buildings too numerous to mention. Perhaps one of the saddest recurring events we recall in the history of Japan's gardens is the destruction of its huge and elaborate pavilions by fire. Most have been reconstructed, but it is difficult if not impossible to duplicate their historical grandeur and importance.

This work is not designed to give the average North American garden aficionado an imperative to replicate the efforts of those who have constructed pavilions previously. Indeed, the design shown in **4-1** would intimidate all but the most zealous carpenter. I offer this chapter more as

inspiration than perspiration. Enjoy these few glimpses of some of the world's greatest examples of Japanese architecture and wood joinery construction. I suspect that if I started construction on a grand pavilion such as this in my backyard nursery, I might be considered quite mad. I also suspect I might get a visit from the city building code and construction permit people. The inspiration to create a gathering place, rather, will most likely be directed toward a deck, barbecue pit, or hot tub enclosure. One can draw ideas of form and architectural detail from these many ancient Japanese structures.

Glean from the pavilion what you can use in a practical, yet suitable, design. Discard the unnecessary grandeur and expense. For those of you who are practicing architects, plans can be obtained through university exchange with the Orient, in library archives, or from Japanese garden architects.

4-1

Construction Close-up

A corner detail of a small pavilion is shown in **4-2**. From this photograph we can get lots of construction ideas for smaller garden structures that we might find in Japanese gardens located in North America. A good carpenter can copy quite faithfully the support structure and construction detail from a photograph such as this. Remember that finished lumber in Japan is planed to metric dimensions, and it will require some adjustment on your part to specify pieces in terms of inches and feet. In addition, Westerners will have to take into account that a nominal two-by-four is actually planed to a dimension of 1⅝ inches by 3⅝ inches.

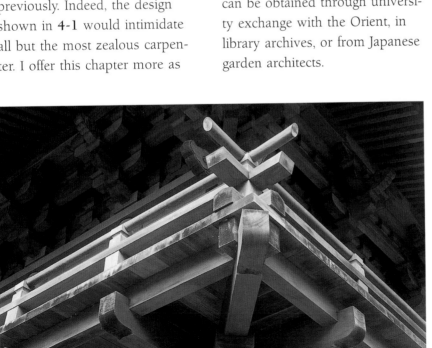

4-2

Pinus thunbergiana, Japanese black pine

Rhododendron satsuki 'Hybrid,' pink gumpo azalea

Three nicely layered Japanese black pines and two large rhododendron frame the flat stone walkway leading to this elevated gazebo. The ground cover can simply be moss.

4-3

Most Japanese construction I have seen in North America utilizes kiln-dried western red cedar, Alaskan yellow cedar, or redwood, depending on availability and suitability for finished color. The blond-colored interior panels commonly found on sliding shoji screens are most often Alaskan yellow cedar. The detail shown in **4-2** is, most likely, western red cedar. The color is a light reddish brown when new, and it fades naturally over time to a silver-gray in bright sunlight. Posts, gates, and decks exposed to the ground or humid conditions are best constructed of redwood. The dark red color, when new, can be stained brown after a few months, if desired. Redwood will also tend to turn silver in the sun as it ages, but make sure that it does not crack open as natural oils are lost. Coat annually with oil or other water-resisting coatings available at your lumber supplier.

A Simple Roof

A pleasing Western treatment of a Japanese roof is shown in **4-3**. The addition of a cupola to the apex adds detail reminiscent of the stacked roofs in elaborate pavilions. The top windows act as skylights to the interior, and provide ventilation for the structure. The cupola thus performs the same functions that ancient structures accomplished with an opening in the roof. Such structures as the Japanese farmhouse used to be open to the sky to let out the smoke from the cooking fire. There was no chimney as such. The copper bottom edge of the roof here provides an aesthetic change of materials and texture from the plain shingles above.

Painted Wood

Many structures are painted in the Japanese garden. The color of red shown in **4-4** is sometimes called Chinese red since it is seen widely in China as well. It is a traditional color associated with shrines, temples, and religious gates.

A bone-colored background and shiny gold details can brighten up a dull garden in a hurry.

Make sure that the red color is not a fire-engine red, and that it has a low gloss. Historically, the gold color was gold plate or hammered gold leaf, so use a very shiny true metallic gold color for the filigree.

Residential Application

Japanese architecture, as I have said, can be successfully utilized in traditional Western homes if it is applied with some restraint. The home shown in **4-5** with the attached garden shed gives the visitor a pleasant combination of Western and Eastern styles. The roof is only partially tiled with accent pieces on the apex and corners. Light use of shoji panels suggests the older style of sliding or removable Japanese screens. The fine stone pathway is a welcome sight to the garden's casual stroller.

4-4

4-5

4-6

THE TEAHOUSE

The Ceremony

One cannot think of the teahouse in a Japanese garden without thinking of the tea ceremony. It is a sacred ritual that eventually involves a sip of tea. For newcomers to the ceremony, the process may seem prolonged, traditional, and a bit complex. The ceremony itself is very structured, even choreographed. There are a strict number of elements, and the age-old gestures and rhythm of the arms seem more like a constrained dance to the Western eye. With study and a careful artistic eye, one can begin to comprehend the importance of these movements. Of course, a complete study of the tea ceremony in a gardening text is unnecessary and does not do justice to this most complex of Japanese rituals. I mention the ceremony in deep respect and choose to leave its complexities to a work focused on its special place in Japanese culture and spirituality.

The teahouse itself is a place where this ceremony might take place. A smaller, isolated structure, as already seen in **4-5** on page 65, is usually reserved for this purpose in the traditional Japanese garden. In Western terms, meaning no disrespect, the teahouse often refers to a small structure in the garden where one might sit in the shade, under cover, and enjoy a beverage and light snack such as cookies or

4-7

individual cakes. One can relax with a conversation while overlooking a pond or a stream. Often the windows are open to important garden scenes. One window might open toward an arched bridge, another might allow the glimpse of a waterfall. Western tradition might call the structure a gazebo or viewing cottage.

The teahouse in **4-6** has a partially hidden path leading to its special place. Once there, you can leave your troubles behind.

Ancient Construction

A detail of the construction of a very old traditional Japanese tea house is shown in **4-7**. It is constructed of nothing but old-growth cryptomeria posts bound with raffia. There are no nails, pegs, or glue holding this sacred structure together. The windows are shuttered against the snow and the hole in the peak of the thatched roof is protected only by being located downwind of the prevailing air currents.

The Cooking Fire

Inside this same ancient structure, noodles and pork are boiled to create a broth (*see* **4-8**). Another back kettle, suspended over the fire, steams bamboo shoots and ginger root. Boiling water is added to the colorful teapot to brew green tea for the guests. The smoke curls up slowly toward the small opening above. It lingers for a moment, giving the house a warm atmosphere of hardwood and cooking spice. Even after a thousand years this special place is still relaxing, cozy, and inviting to the soul. Upon leaving, you look back over your shoulder longingly as the evening comes to a close.

4-8

MIXING STYLES

A Chinese Structure in the Japanese Garden

Many garden designers may prefer to keep the style in their garden uniform and subtle in its expression. But there is much precedent for utilizing whatever elements appeal to you the most. If this means mixing styles between periods of Japanese history or drawing from other traditions such as Korean or Chinese, then that is up to you.

Since my objective is to assist you in creating your own peaceful space, my preference is for the quiet, subtle beauty of the understated Japanese styles. In certain settings, however, a flashier style may be fine.

A Chinese-style gazebo is seen in **4-9** situated in a cultivated Japanese garden. It is bright and flashy by comparison to the Japanese styles. The curved tile roof has some familiarity to the traditional style, but the elaborate bright white and red paint are more reminiscent of earlier periods in Oriental history (*refer to* **4-4**). I offer the image in **4-9** as an alternative to the more subtle, understated teahouses we see most often. One can immediately see the resemblance to the Victorian garden gazebo with its six sides, central location, high degree of filigree, prominent white color, and its views in all directions. A traditional tea ceremony would be inappropriate in this structure.

4-9

The simple construction and design of a miniature teahouse that functions as a lantern can be seen well in **4-10**. The sacred qualities of the structure are demystified. Simple construction like this that mimics architectural elements is sometimes used to camouflage various utilitarian structures such as pump houses, birdfeeders, and mailboxes as well as rest rooms and telephone booths. This is in no way meant to belittle the sacred tea ceremony; it is simply a way to hide the mundane from view in an otherwise unspoiled garden. Its simple lines and construction are highly useful for myriad uses in the Western variation of the Japanese garden.

4-10

Acer japonicum 'Aconitifolium,' *full moon maple*

Acer palmatum, Japanese maple, red pygmy

MOON VIEWING

The moon-viewing structure is by day bright and open (*see* **4-11**), and is located where the normal path of the moon can be reflected on the water below. There is ample, comfortable seating to accommodate a prolonged stay.

Cushions are brought to the site to ease relaxation and to encourage quiet conversation and contemplation. Special racks will hold your favorite hot or cold beverage. This is quiet time for introspection and philosophy. Discussions are not lively, nor are they argumentative. Mutual

respect is given others as they, perhaps, search their souls for some higher meaning. I enjoyed a fine moon with some Japanese friends in just such a place, as I recorded in **4-12**, on page 72. In the spirit of that special night, I wrote the poem on page 73 in their moon-viewing room.

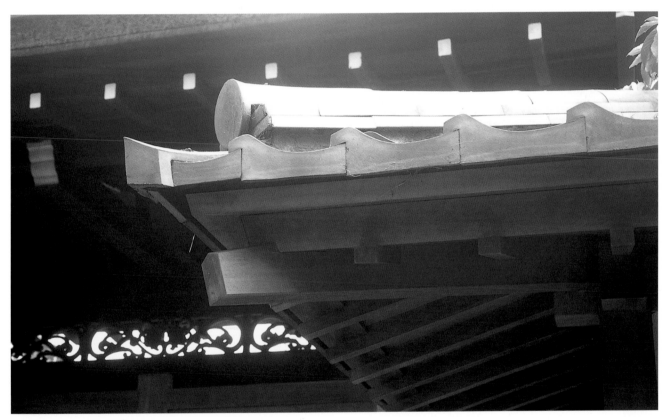

4-11

Acer palmatum, Japanese maple, garnet

Acer japonicum 'Aconitifolium,' full moon maple

Dark lily pad mosaics before sunrise

draw their sustenance and support

from the cold black pond waters

of the first day of spring.

Only now are the earliest sparkling

reflections of dawn so distinct.

They offer a profound parable

for new beginnings.

Herb L. Gustafson

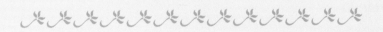

chapter 5

GARDEN ORNAMENTS

The sound is similar to what you hear in underground caves that still contain an active river. **Suikinkutsu** *translates as "water harp chamber."*

The traditional Japanese garden brings to the viewer a vast array of symbolic representations. These can be a seemingly simple element such as a fence or as subtle as the arrangement of boulders, paths, streams, and waterfalls. Here I present specific garden ornaments.

THE BASIN STONE

The *Chozubachi*

The *chozubachi*—literally water basin—is located near the garden gate. As shown in **5-1**, it offers the visitor a refreshing drink of water. This basin stone is large enough to lean on to rest. The trickle of water coming from the bamboo spout makes a pleasant sound as it hits the center of the hand-hewn basin. Guests may drink from the bamboo ladle lying across the water, or simply touch the water with a few fingertips and stroke their foreheads to cool the sensitive area between the eyes. By such a gesture, we relax away the worries of the day and cleanse our minds for the upcoming journey down the garden path. There are many Zen rituals that encourage us to "turn the page." There is a suggestion of forgiveness in this practice; we are reminded that whatever events were in our immediate past are now beyond our control or concern. We mark the moment we decide to let go by touching our tense, furrowed brow with the cleansing water spirit of the *chozubachi*.

5-1

The Well

Water plays an important role in the Japanese garden. It obviously forms the waterfalls, streams, and ponds, and, as an offering to the human spirit, water takes on additional meaning. Both in practical and spiritual terms, water is the giver of life. It is one of the fundamental elements of the Buddhist philosophy of Creation and it is also suggested in many other religions of the world. The offer of refreshment to the weary traveler is seen in **5-2**. Often, visits to the Japanese garden are leisurely but will span a period of a few hours. When the body says that a moist wipe across the forehead is inadequate, this well will look very appealing. The falling leaves are kept out by a fine grid of bamboo canes lashed together with raffia. To assure retrieval, the cedar bucket is firmly attached to the vertical pole behind the cairn. Notice the seating stones nearby in the shade.

The Ornamental Basin

The carved stone boat shown in **5-3** is a fine example of an ornamental-type basin. Notice the absence of the bamboo dripping vessel or a cedar bucket. The water is allowed to grow lilies or other floating ornamental plants. The arrangement is for viewing pleasure only.

Large stones can be carved in the shape of frogs, turtles, fish, or any aquatic-related object, such as this boat. Sometimes a large, highly decorative ceramic pot is used.

These accoutrements of the garden remind us of the life—other than our own—that is sustained by water.

5-2

5-3

Rain-catching Stones

Originating in China as a form of *P'en J'ing*, special stones that reminded scholars of natural scenery or objects were collected and displayed. One classification emerged as the "water stone." These stones, some quite large, had natural hollows that reminded the viewer of a high lake surrounded by mountains or a glacier-fed valley below a snow-capped peak. Natural crystalline enclosures in the rock could suggest streams, waterfalls, or snow. Japan enjoyed the art of viewing these special stones and call it *suiseki*. Large natural *suiseki* are prized in the Japanese garden as symbols of the ultimate water source. Their natural hollows collect rainwater and give back to us the illusion of a miniature world within the garden (*see* **5-4**).

5-4

The *Tsukubai*

The *tsukubai* is distinguished from the *chozubachi* by its height. The lower elevation of a *tsukubai* water basin requires the partaker to bend a bit to reach the water. This carved stone basin (*see* **5-5**) is placed on a low, flat rock. It is not as elevated as the previous water basins (compare with **5-1**). The act of bending down towards the water becomes an act of supplication and reverence. The lack of a dipper here suggests that this water is for the soul only and one must bend his or her knee a bit to receive its blessing. This water arrangement suggests that you are entering a sacred portion of the garden—perhaps the outer garden of the teahouse—or approaching a shrine.

5-5

5-6

The *Suikinkutsu*

When you look at the beautiful *tsukubai* shown in **5-6**, you cannot see the *suikinkutsu* below. You can only hear it. The excess water in the basin runs down the forward right edge of the stone and onto the polished pebbles below.

Underneath this basin stone is another large basin made out of a ceramic vase. The water falls an additional distance in the air before plunking down noisily on the water surface of the underground chamber. The sound is similar to what you hear in underground caves that still contain an active river. Suikinkutsu translates as "water harp chamber." The construction of these underground chambers is complex and exacting. One has to literally "tune" the chamber by matching the droplet size, the rate of free-fall, the rate of discharge of excess water, and the volume of the resonating ceramic chamber.

For a rough cutaway diagram showing the relationship between the *tsukubai* and the *suikinkutsu*, see the drawing below. Note that the water harp has a close relationship to the shorter water basins, and not the larger greeting-type basins found at the front garden gate. Note also the absence of the dipper; these water harps are used in conjunction with sacred places and are for meditative purposes only.

Another fine water harp is hidden under the low basin in **5-7**. Here you can clearly see the large pebbles that catch the excess water from the top basin. You

5-7

can often detect the presence of the *suikinkutsu* by the absence of a visible drain to accommodate the pouring water. The drain is underground. Just as apparent,

however, is the difference in sound. Spend a little extra time around one of these amazing garden basins. The sound is unique and fulfilling.

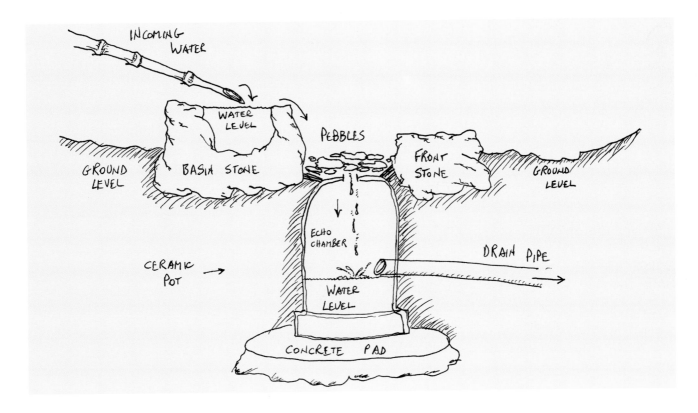

5-8

The Deer Chaser

One of my favorite garden ornaments is the so-called deer chaser
(*see* **5-8**), although it does not
actually chase deer away. I have
seen deer grazing on boxwood
just a few steps away from one
of these devices. I suspect the
name simply comes from the
rather load "knock" it makes on a
regular basis. I also suspect it is
more effective at keeping away
moles or attracting children.
Maybe that's how the deer get
chased. Anyway, water pours
from a bamboo spout just as in

the chozubachi, except that the
water pours into another hollowed section of bamboo. The
weight of the water tips this bamboo stick down; it swivels on an
axis fixed to the ground. Once
the bamboo tilts down and
dumps its load of water into the
basin, it returns with a knock
into its original position. It is a
rather clever and interesting time-
piece.

Buddhist monks used to use a
device like this to mark the passage of time during meditation.
The "clunk" became, at once,
both the beginning and the end

of a block of time. Earlier, I men-
tioned the importance of the
moistened fingertip on the forehead as the ending time of worry
and the commencement of the
rest of your life. For the meditation ritual, monks would use the
knock as the ending of one
thought and the beginning of
another. These thoughts were a
part of a pre-set series of topics
that had been accepted as proper
focus and preparation for con-
templative control. Much as one
shifts to the next bead on a
rosary, the monk shifted to the
next memorized mind focus. The

meditative experience was thus broken vertically by the beginnings and endings of all these bits of time, but the larger horizontal picture of total content fused it all together.

I remember well a conversation I had with Andrés Segovia, the legendary guitarist. When I asked him if he was ever frustrated with the guitar being plucked rather than bowed, he replied with great thought, "The guitar is a vertical instrument like the harpsichord." He made a chopping motion in the air with his hand. "One pluck ends the note before it and begins the one after. Only when you look back at the musical phrase they collectively created do you know whether you have succeeded or not." The deer chaser was like that to Zen thought. We can look back at the results of our tiny efforts and judge for ourselves their worth.

GARDEN SCULPTURE

Cranes

The two cranes shown in **5-9** are an example of some of the garden sculpture associated with the Japanese garden.

Cranes are long-lived birds and, along with the tortoise, wish the visitor the same. The bronze sculptures are positioned here in the shallows, just as they would naturally be found. The two different postures and their relationship help make the scene very real. Subtle sculpture such as this can add to our enjoyment of the garden. I have seen tasteful uses for frogs, tortoises, turtles, salamanders, and even fish. Make the scene as natural as possible. Watch carefully for accuracy of scale, habitat, posture, and site surroundings. Avoid overuse, garish color, and out-of-place animals.

Western gardens might benefit from herons rather than cranes, raccoons rather than tortoises. An out-of-character sculpture detracts rather than adds to the garden design.

5-9

5-10

effect is still there but perhaps more subtle. I suspect that garden owners may suit themselves when arranging or designing these pieces into their garden scheme. This unobtrusive seated figure does a nice job of reminding me of the source of much Japanese thought and philosophy, other than strict religious dogma. I have seen huge figures, hundreds of feet tall, that purposely overwhelm the area around them. You can see these statues towering over buildings. I suggest that in a Western garden these might be a bit garish. I once was taking a picture of one of these statues, when a teenage boy crawled out of the ear, giving me at once a shock of disbelief and an immediate sense of scale!

Deer

The impish-looking deer in **5-10** adds a smile to the garden stroller. The face is mythological and Pan-like. It reminds me of the Eden in *niwa*. I can imagine following this playful animal back into the bamboo thicket behind and coming across a lost world of fanciful creatures, leprechauns, and unicorns—a nice repast along our garden journey.

Religious Symbols

Normally, the use of symbols, such as the seated Buddha in **5-11**, is reserved for special places, such as a shrine. Occasionally, one comes across figures, figurines, busts, heads, and other religious symbols in spare number in the Japanese garden. The figure of the Buddha is most often seen as a sentinel stone in a boulder arrangement, where the

5-11

5-12

STONE LANTERNS

Cast Concrete

A typical design for a cast-concrete lantern is shown in **5-12**. Freshly mixed cement and water is poured into a mold and allowed to set. Simple lanterns are cast in one piece and are very small and inexpensive. More elaborate lanterns can be made by stacking individually cast sections on top of one another. This style is actually four different pieces: the four-legged base, the flat stand above it, the hollow lantern portion, and finally the top cap. More elaborate structures are available as multitiered pagoda-styled lanterns similar to those in **5-16** and **5-17**. The advantage of concrete is the price. There are some drawbacks, however. Concrete lanterns are more porous than stone, so, in freezing weather, they are apt to chip and crack. And the concrete has a tendency to age badly. At first, the high-alkaline surface will not allow the growth of moss or lichens. A few sprays of buttermilk will lower the pH a bit and add a film of nutrition on which airborne moss spores can start. Unfortunately, as with our concrete driveways and patios, the aging process sometimes gets out of hand and we get green slimy algae forming in a few years.

These can be cleaned off fairly quickly with a spray of 50 percent household bleach and water; but then the moss is killed and the nice lichens as well.

Stone can be carved to show fine detail that cannot be duplicated in cast concrete. I have seen fine stone lanterns where the screen mesh covering the light chamber was actually carved out of a single stone. Concrete couldn't possibly have that much detail. This design is perhaps one of the most widely seen in the Japanese garden. Its low shape and wide cap are best viewed under a few inches of snow; hence, the name *yukimi doro*, or snow lantern (see 5-12).

Carved Stone

The rather tall and delicately carved stone lantern in **5-13** has a post-type stand that suggests a heron or a crane standing on one leg; hence, the name *nure sagi*. The cap is carved in the shape of the lotus blossom. Notice the fine detail around the light chamber.

This very old lantern is covered with prized blue-green lichens. This epiphyte grows slowly, about 80 years, to make a spot the size of a U.S. silver dollar. Its presence is revered, as are all ancient things in Japan. This lantern has only the suggestion of a light chamber, represented by the carved circular indentation on all four sides.

We see many examples of symbolism in the Japanese garden. One of the basic Buddhist elements is fire, and the lantern not only lights our paths but symbolizes the beginnings of the earth by fire and the formative power of volcanoes. It is an easy stretch of the imagination to allow an unlit lantern to guide our paths during the day; so, why not have a lantern that only reminds us of the power of light? We have gravel oceans, bronze birds, and stone Buddhas; so

why not unlit lanterns? Notice the single post. This type of post is simply a temple-type stand that we find supporting markers and items of interest.

Another basic Buddhist symbol that we see in the Japanese garden is the lotus flower. The single-post stand in **5-13** holds up an unopened lotus blossom (compare this with the open style in **5-14**). Again, we see the crusty lichens on the cap or umbrella. This is a typical four-legged lantern although the bushes hide it. The four legs are typically carved to look like a lion's or a tiger's, or sometimes

5-13

5-14

just the claws. Lanterns that have only two feet are known as *kotoji doro*, which means koto tuner. The koto is the Japanese harp; the instrument is tuned by listening to a tone produced by a standard two-pronged metal fork as it is struck. The two legs are usually planted one on land, the other in water, to celebrate the musical and philosophical interdependence of these two elements. The stand holds up an open lotus flower. Actual lotus blossums are often grown in the Japanese garden as well, as seen in **5-15**.

5-15

Multitiered

The three stacked lanterns seen in **5-16** are collectively called the *sambon-noto*. The three light chambers represent earth, water, and sky. The lantern sits on the four legs of a lion representing strength. The nine rings at the top are symbols of the nine heavens in the Buddhist pantheon. The very top lotus blossom is a representation of the Buddha. As you can see, stone lanterns can tell a story, offer spiritual advice, and guide our footsteps in the right direction. In a way, the stone lantern symbolizes "symbolism" in the Japanese garden. Its shape, structure, and position are meaningful. When you are planning your garden, take care to place your lanterns where they are just as meaningful to you.

5-16

The imposing multitiered pagoda shown in **5-17** is of contemporary design. The protruding square "rooftops" contain nine stories of light. The pattern above that is the already familiar nine circles of heaven capped by the lotus blossom. This fairly new pagoda is constructed of machined granite. Some hand-carved details can be seen on the top cap. The structure guards the entrance to a holy garden.

Bronze

A fine example of a bronze lantern is shown in **5-18**. It is weathering nicely to the gray-green patina seen in many copper-containing metal alloys. It should never be polished. These lanterns can be lit easily by running a low-voltage cord through their hollow base. Stone and concrete lanterns are more difficult to wire and are usually just left as they are. I have wired cast-concrete lanterns by drilling a hole through the center of each stacked piece with a concrete drill and threading a wire through to a dim lamp inside the light chamber. Low voltage is best because of the risk of shock. An inexpensive transformer and timer, plugged into your exterior electrical outlet, are all you need to power your wire. The timer can be replaced with a photoelectric switch, if desired. The lantern will then automatically turn on at dusk and off at dawn. The lantern can even be hooked up to a motion sensor for security.

5-17

5-18

Seating Stones

The nicely carved stones shown in **5-19** and **5-20** can function as seating for the weary visitor, or can be used as a fine base for a decorative vase of flowers. A stone like one of these can support a great deal of weight, and is perfect for large bonsai in the garden. Imagine a 30-inch round earthenware pot on a stone stand containing a five-foot-tall, picturesque, 100-year-old pine tree. For best positioning, set the stone where it gets natural shade at about two o'clock in the afternoon. That way, it will be sunny when the temperature is cool and

5-19

5-20

shady as the afternoon heats up. This condition is good for preserving the stone, making a visitor comfortable sitting on it, placing a vase of cut flowers, or displaying a fine old potted tree.

BENCHES

Benches are found in the garden at the top of a hill; after a long series of steps; in front of a waterfall; by the garden gate or by a well. Benches offer a convenient resting place for a moment of meditation and/or given an opportunity to view a special place in a prolonged fashion.

On Top of a Retaining Wall

The bench shown in **5-21** is merely some wooden planks that top a retaining wall. The slope is held back by the stone construction and is capped by a simple cedar bench top. The stone rounds the near corner into a sunnier location, providing the user with a choice of sun or shade: wood or stone bench. The "U"-shaped design provides a group of several people with the chance to engage in pleasant conversation.

5-21

A Log Bench

The simple bench shown in **5-22** is hewn out of a cedar log. The sturdy legs and back are attached by glue and pegs. This stout structure can be moved if necessary, yet it offers a sense of permanence to the scene. The cedar will eventually turn a nice silver-gray color that will blend with the green of the foliage behind it, as well as with the gray of the granite walkway in front. An annual application of linseed oil each summer will keep the large timbers from cracking and warping.

5-22

5-23

The Slatted Bench

The top surface of the bench shown in **5-23** is constructed of many slats. This bench is a fine example of Japanese joinery. The slats will drain well after a sudden downpour, so the seating surface will dry almost immedi-ately. The "U"-shaped design pro-motes conversation, and the lack of a backrest allows the user to hang his or her legs over either the front, back, or sides to enjoy the view in all directions.

Note the smaller portable bench in the background. This can be brought over near the largest bench to serve as a tea stand or snack table. This type of construction would work well on a back deck or for a place where you want to cool down between dips in a spa. A rolling barbecue grill could turn your seating area into a gathering place for guests.

BRIDGES

The Covered Bridge

Bridges are functional structures that allow us to cross a stream or narrow body of water. These devices, as practical as they may be, still symbolize an important transition in the Japanese garden path. The stroller is offered a special view over water, and we are inclined to stay awhile at the center. The covered bridge in **5-24** is both beautiful and functional. In inclement weather we can linger there for a longer time. We are protected from the rain in a sudden downpour as well as offered a bench in a shady spot over the water on a hot, sunny day. The architecture of the cover blends nicely with the rest of the garden and its structures. We are reminded of the passage through the front garden gate, with its welcoming roof and offer of shelter, seating, and water. In philosophical terms, we are also reminded of the English expression "We will cross that bridge when we come to it." A similar Japanese expression allows us the opportunity to view the crossing as a milestone on our life's journey. In essence, it says to us that

5-24

5-25

we have made it this far. Do we want to turn back? Do we wish to continue on the same path or change directions? We do indeed cross that bridge, but only when we get there. We pause a moment to reflect on our journey thus far. The reflection we get back from the water below allows us to see ourselves as we really are. Then we move on.

The Strolling Pond Bridge

The inviting path to the large pond gives us a wonderfully far-away view of the nicely curved bridge seen in **5-25**.

Notice how the reflection in the water appears to exaggerate the bridge's curvature just slightly. One path invites us to the water's edge; another, to our right, beckons us to seek out access to the distant bridge. We are invited by the water to linger at both.

5-26

The Moon Bridge

Highly arched bridges can form a complete circle for the viewer from a distance, when one considers the top arch and its reflection below. The bridge in **5-26**, at the left, forms only a portion of a circle, and therefore would form an incomplete circular form upon reflection. This photograph has neither the proper angle nor the light conditions to show a reflection in the stream below. The form that would be shaped by the reflection—a partial circle—is viewed as a phase of the moon rather than no moon at all.

Observe closely the fine combination of logs, planks, and curved timbers used in construction. At night, the reflection of the "moon" and the lantern make this a very special view.

5-27

The arch of the bridge may also form a special realtionship not just with the water below, but also, perhaps, with a stream-side path that curves away in the distance, as in **5-27**.

A Simple Stone Slab

A quarried and cut slice of granite laid across a narrow stream is shown in **5-28**. The two stream edges are reinforced with stone for stability and erosion control. A larger cluster of stones is placed to one side to create an asymmetry that counters the dominant symmetry of the simple stone slab structure. Notice the handrail at the right edge that offers security for the step down from the slab.

5-28

5-29

Acer palmatum 'Shishigushira,' Japanese maple

A Log Bridge

For the woodland natural garden stream shown in **5-29**, a simple log bridge fits in quite well. Log supports below are pretreated with preservatives to help them last longer in the water. A layer of short logs is then placed on two long logs—which is much like laying ties under a railroad track. The vertical rise is small, so no handrails are present. Wooden structures such as this need annual attention. Remove algae and moss with a light spray of bleach diluted in water, and when it is hot and dry in the summer, apply a coat of linseed oil to minimize cracking and drying of the posts.

chapter 6

GARDEN DESIGN

Untrimmed trees, wood-land paths, and meander-ing streams are combined so that one gets a feeling of being in the woods in the natural garden style, **shukei yen.**

THINGS TO CONSIDER

When we compare the Japanese garden with the English or common Western garden, a few similarities and many differences emerge. The English country estate garden tends to be quite showy in its floral display. The Japanese garden has few flowers (*see* **6-1**). English gardens have many geometric shapes reiterated in their cottages, gazebos, hedges, fountains, and sundials. The Japanese garden abhors symmetry, and prefers the delicate balance of gently skewed arrangements of rocks and trees in odd numbers. No path is straight and no two garden sculptures are identical. Even the two great cats that guard the gate are male and female in appropriate posture and size. The English flower borders and wildflower meadows are intended to convey a bright natural world filled with every imaginable size, shape, color, texture, and scent of nature's splendor. The Japanese garden attempts to reach deeper into our powers of sensation and perception.

The Japanese have always felt that one lotus blossom floating on a chartreuse lily pad in the middle of a clear, still pond offers the viewer a greater degree of profundity and inner examination than the overwhelming riot of color favored by most Westerners. This type of experience must be felt firsthand by the garden observer. No visitor to some of Japan's greatest gardens will go away disappointed.

6-1

But to understand the physiological and psychological processes at work in our minds is a necessary first step in making our own Japanese garden. The Japanese garden is not simply an assortment of curved bridges, pagodas, bronze cranes, and poodle pines. We cannot make a sea by just raking the sand. Rather, we first visit the site with our minds and creative spirit open to laying out a design that takes into account the natural lay of the land, type of stones, appropriate plant material, and concern for maintenance.

What follows is a brief description of five popular Japanese garden styles along with some drawings of possible designs. Study each of them and choose the appropriate style to suit your site. Only in large garden areas would I risk trying to combine two or more of these styles. I have found that most Western backyard areas are simply not big enough to do this successfully without clutter or crowding.

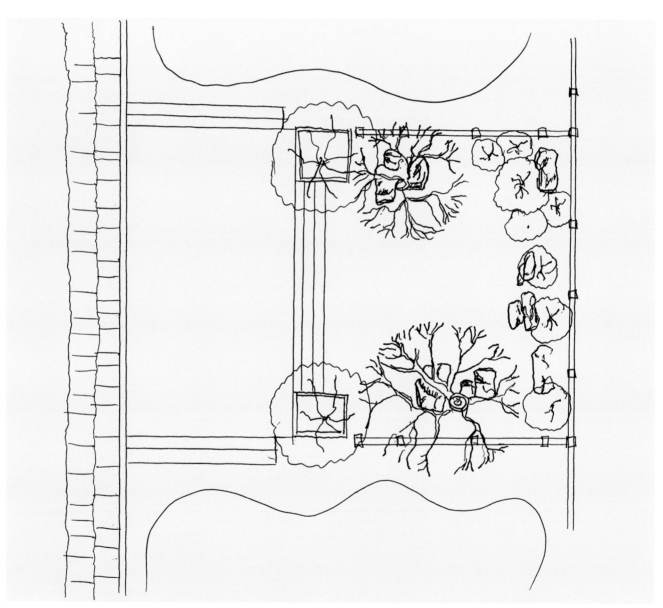

An ordinary back patio can be easily converted into a garden stage where the visitor can view an enclosed courtyard toward the back fence. Additional side fences, right and left, provide a nice backdrop for a small private garden, leaving the rest of the backyard for more practical uses, such as a lawn play area or vegetable garden.

6-2

FIVE JAPANESE GARDENS

The Strolling Pond Garden

The strolling pond garden, *chisen-kaiyu-skiki*, contains a flat, still pond of irregular outline (*see* **6-2**) as its primary feature.

A path meanders around its circumference with side trips up to adjacent grassy knolls, lookouts, and down to the water's edge. The pond is crossed at its narrow points by the curved moon bridge. Large stones partially submerged in the water represent the crane or tortoise, depending on their natural shape or posture. They wish the visitor a long life. Here we also find the heron garden sculptures in a still inlet. A bronze frog may be taking in the sun on top of a flat stone at the shoreline. The stone lantern of choice would be the two-legged *kotoji doro*, with one leg in the water and the other leg on land.

A marshy inlet might support a few hundred Japanese iris. A weeping willow could be planted so that it hangs over the deepest pool. Water lilies provide shade and cover for the koi.

The Flat Sea Garden

This type of garden is called *hiraniwa* and features a flat expanse of raked sand or fine gravel that represents the sea. A portion of a temple that incorporates the walkways into the graveled areas is shown in **6-3**.

At the gravel edge, a rake is used to suggest waves at the shoreline. In most flat gardens, walkways do not proceed out into the raked sand area. Benches provide points for rest and contemplation. Stones and boulders are placed halfway out into the raked area to simulate a shoreline. "Islands" may appear as mounded plantings in the "sea." Sometimes a parable may be told by the placement of stones in the raked area, similar to that done in the sand-and-stone garden, but without the wall enclosure. This style is best known for its profuse use of layered Japanese black pines as a backdrop. Lower shrubs, hedges, and small flowering trees provide the medium-distance view on the other side of the sand.

The Natural Garden

An example of the natural garden style, *shukei yen*, is shown in **6-4**. The main feature of this style is to put together untrimmed trees, woodland paths, and meandering streams so that one gets a feeling of being in the woods. Lots of soft shades of green make up the tall background and tree canopy above. These gardens often utilize moss as the primary ground cover. There is spare use of lanterns or curving bridges. Often, water is crossed by stepping on a few flat stones in the stream. We see a heavy use of ferns, bamboo, pieris, rhododendron, azaleas, dogwood, nandina, fatsia, and other shade-loving plants. We see few pines, koi, flowers or other plants that have high light requirements.

6-3

6-4

Many backyards have a pair of matching mature trees that were planted when the house was built. This design allows the visitor to travel across the existing patio to a raised deck at the far fence line. The views of these large trees then become individual, rather than twin. This breaks up the symmetry that would limit the Japanese garden scheme.

The Tea Garden

The tea garden, *rojiniwa*, usually surrounds the ceremonial tea-house. This area is usually divided further into an outer entrance garden (*see* **6-5**) and a sacred inner garden which the guests are not allowed to enter, but only observe from a low window or deck (*see* **6-6**).

The outer garden will have a welcoming water basin, a narrow crooked path, and a half-open gate with a suspended overhead beam that forces the visitor to bow his or her head when entering and leaving.

The inner garden will likely have a small water focus such as the deer chaser, dry well, or water harp.

The inner garden often displays a single bonsai on a stand. A low interior shelf will have a simple ikebana, or flower arrangement. Simple scrolls may display haiku or landscape brush painting to complement the inner garden. A suiseki, or viewing stone, suggests the rocky environment from which the bonsai comes.

This is a simple courtyard scheme that might be part of a larger tea garden or might be adopted where space does not afford the layout of a full Japanese garden design. A tiled roof fence makes a suitable backdrop for a cluster of rocks, a tall Japanese maple, and a clump of nadina or heavenly bamboo. An exterior hung scroll of calligraphy can be exhibited for expected guests or rendered on glass for a more permanent display.

6-5

6-6

For a home with large natural trees and a wooded side lot, this idea with an elevated teahouse works well. The mature trees can be any native hardwood such as oak, beech, birch, walnut or similar. The raked sand is kept at a bit of a distance from the falling leaves, to ease maintenance. A fine tilted Japanese laceleaf maple is planted on a small rock "island," and it is very visible from the path or a bench in the teahouse.

Acer palmatum 'Dissectum,' Japanese laceleaf maple

Acer palmatum, Japanese maple seedling

The Sand & Stone Garden

One corner of a typical sand-and-stone garden, or *seki tei*, is shown in **6-7**. Also see the photo to the right, previously seen as **2-7**, to see another similar garden. The sand-and-stone garden is walled. Without this wall, your eyes are distracted by the distant view. In the flat tea garden, the wall is replaced by a tall, dense hedge of horizontally pruned pine trees. The sand is usually coarser than common beach sand, for stability in windy or rainy weather. A

Stone-and-sand garden with a wall, previously seen as 2-7

6-7

coarse granite or quartz grit will rake easily, hold its shape well, and offers a light color that resembles the light reflecting off the sea.

The stones are positioned to tell a tale of a famous battle or to portray a legendary dragon. Often, the tallest rock is a sentinel stone that symbolizes the Buddha. (Refer again to the photo on page 103, previously seen as **2-7**.) The smaller stones often represent accompanying children, young animals, smaller forest creatures, or fictitious elves or pranksters. The symbolism is meant to be profound and philosophical, and an observation bench is provided for prolonged meditation.

A simple idea for the treatment of a small side area next to the entrance to the garage or workshop. This low-maintenance solution contains only a nicely trimmed white pine, hardy heath, and an andromeda. Some bulbs or perennials can be planted so that they peek out from underneath the rocks in spring. Five boulders and raked sand make up the nonliving portion of this planting.

Acer palmatum 'Bloodgood,' Japanese maple

Cedrus atlanticus 'Glauca pendula,' Atlas cedar

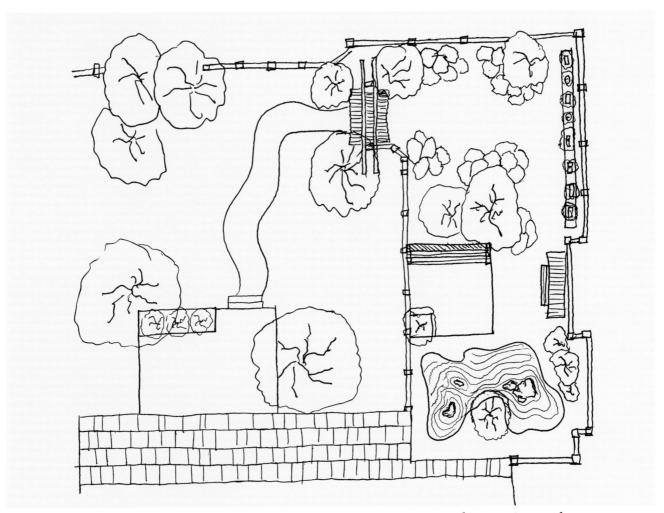

This side-yard design offers the homeowner an opportunity to isolate varying garden uses. The typical back patio leads to a curving path out of sight. The guest is led past bonsai shelves from the entrance gate and a growing area for potential bonsai growing in the ground. A work station is positioned against the outside fence and a second patio or viewing station overlooks the private sand-and-stone garden.

TRAINING METHODS

Plants are trained and shaped either by using copper wire, raffia, bamboo stakes, or by pruning. Often we can utilize a combination of all these methods to maximize our results in a minimum of time. A typical slanting-style pine tree in a container similar to a large bonsai is shown in 6-8. This plant has had its branches and trunk shaped by winding annealed copper wire around the areas that need shaping. Gentle pressure with the hands, or assisted with clamps, the branches are bent.

The wire may be cut off after a year's time. Larger branches may require several years' training. Remove the wire before it cuts into the bark. A golden yew and green pine are shown in 6-9, trained entirely by pruning and hedging. There are many outline shapes found in the Japanese garden that resemble ovals, flat-topped hedges, squared-off sides, flame-shaped bushes, and serpentine-topped border planting. A simple hedge trimmer is often all you need.

6-8

6-9

A typical cloud formation as applied to a juniper is shown in **6-10**. The interior of the plant is cut away to expose the inner trunk and main branches. The outer branches are then layered into this cloud-shaped shrub. To avoid the common "poodle" effect, avoid pruning your "clouds" into ball-shaped branches. A group of junipers that have been trimmed to exaggerate their

weeping style is shown in **6-11**. The upper branches have been exposed by trimming and the downward-facing branches have been let go to encourage their weight and visual mass.

A typical pine branch that is being layered out horizontally along some bamboo stakes is shown in **6-12**. The branches are lightly tied to the bamboo with raffia, which will not scar the

branches as readily as copper wire can. It takes about two years to secure the pine branch into a permanent "cloud" shape or posture. The emerging vertical candles in spring are knocked off by the sharp blow of a long bamboo cane cut longitudinally in half. New candles then appear later in the year, which will thicken and beautify each of the individual branches.

6-10

6-11

6-12

6-13

Chamaecyparis pisifera, golden threadbranch cypress

Acer palmatum 'Lutescens,' Japanese maple

A cluster of small bushes that are being trained by gravity is shown by **6-13**. Look closely, and you can see rocks of all sizes that have been fastened to the lower branches to pull them down. This type of training is gentle but persistent; the force never lets up. Larger branches can be brought down to resemble low alpine branches under a heavy annual snow load.

The tops and sides of these shrubs are pruned with common garden shears and hedge trimmers. Any training method that looks attractive and is effective is suitable in a Japanese garden.

chapter 7

PLANT MATERIALS

Acer palmatum Azuma mursaki, **Japanese maple**

JAPANESE GLOSSARY

Japanese Name	Common Name	Botanical Name
ajisai	hydrangea	Hydrangea spp.
Akamatsu	Japanese red pine	Pinus densiflora
akebi	five-leaf akebia	Akebia quinata
aoki	Japanese aucuba	Aucuba japonica
asebi	lily-of-the-valley bush	Pieris japonica
biwa	loquat	Eriobotrya japonica
botan	peony	Paeonia suffruticosa
cha	tea	Thea sinensis
ebine	calanthe	Calanthe discolor
eurya	sakaki	Cleyera japonica/Sakakia ochnacea/ Eurya ochnacea
fuji	wisteria	Wisteria floribunda
goyomatsu	Japanese white pine	Pinus pentaphylla
hagi	bush clover	Lespedeza bicolor
hinoki	hinoki cypress/white cedar	Chamaecyparis obtusa
hisakaki	eurya	Eurya japonica
ichii	Japanese yew	Taxuz cuspidata
icho	ginkgo/maidenhair	Ginkgo biloba
jinoyoge	winter daphne	Daphne odora
kaki	Japanese persimmon	Diospyros kaki
kakitsu	rabbit-ear iris	Iris laevigata
kashiwagi	konara oak	Quercus glandulifera
katsura	katsura tree	Cercidiphyllum japonicum
keyaki	zelkova	Zelkova serrata
kiri	royal paulownia	Paulownia tomentosa
kirishima	azalea	Rhododendron obtusum
koshi	tangerine	Citrus reticulata
kunugi	sawtooth oak	Quercus acutissima
kuri	chestnut	Castanea creanata
kusunoki	camphor tree	Cinnamomum camphora
kuromatsu	Japanese black pine	Pinus thunbergiana
maki	yew	Podocarpus macrophyllus
masaki	spindle tree	Euonymus japonica

Japanese Name	Common Name	Botanical Name
matsu	pine	*Pinus spp.*
mayumi	spindle tree	*Euonymus kiautschovica*
miyama kirishima	azalea	*Rhododendron kiusianum*
mokkoku	tea camellia	*Camellia sinensis*
mokusei	sweet olive	*Osmanthus fragrans*
momiji/kaede/keikanbok	Japanese maple	*Acer palmatum*
momo	peach	*Prunus persica*
murasa	gromwell	*Lithospermum incisum*
nanten	heavenly bamboo	*Nandina domestica*
nashi	Asian pear	*Pyrus pyrifolia*
nikkei	cinnamon tree	*Cinnamomum sieboldii*
ozasa	bamboo grass	*Sasa veitchii*
renge-tsutsuji	azalea	*Rhododendron japonicum*
sakura	flowering cherry	*Prunus serrulata*
sarusuberi	crape myrtle	*Lagerstroemia indica*
sata tsutsuji	azalea	*Rhododendron sataense*
satuski	azalea	*Rhododendron indicum*
sazanka	sasanqua camellia	*Camellia sasanqua*
sekisho	grassy-leaved sweet flag	*Acorus gramineus*
shiinoki	chinquapin	*Castonopsis cuspidata*

Pinus mugo 'Gnome,' mountain pine

Acer palmatum, Japanese maple seedling

Japanese Name	Common Name	Botanical Name
shion	aster	*Aster tartaricus*
shiragi	white chrysanthemum	*Chrysanthemum morifolium*
sugi	Japanese cedar	*Cryptomeria japonica*
tachibana	mandarin orange	*Citrus reticulata*
take	bamboo	*Phyllostachys* spp.
tsubaki	camellia	*Camellia japonica*
tsutsuji	azalea	*Rhododendron* spp.
ume	Japanese apricot "plum"	*Prunus mume*
wasabi	Japanese horseradish	*Wasabia japonica*
yadome	box-leaved holly	*Ilex crenata*
yamabuki	Japanese rose	*Kerria japonica*
yama urushi	wild sumac	*Rhus trichocoapa*
yama-tsutsuji	torch azalea	*Rhododendron kaempferi*
yamazakura	wild cherry	*Prunus jamasakura*
yanagi	willow	*Salix* spp., esp. *babylonica*
yatsude	Japanese formosa	*Fatsia japonica*
yukitanagi	Thunberg spiraea	*Spiraea thunbergii*
yuzu	citron	*Citrus medica*
yuzuriha	daphniphyllum	*Daphniphyllum macropodum*
zakuro	pomegranate	*Punica granatum*

Rhododendron yakushimanum 'Yaku angel,'
rhododendron

Rhodendron satsuki 'Hybrid,'
pink gumpo azalea

PLANTS GROUPED BY USE

Large Background Trees, Evergreen

LATIN	COMMON
Cedrus	cedar
Cinnamomum camphora	camphor tree
Pinus nigra	Austrian black pine
Pinus thunbergiana	Japanese black pine
Pinus wallichiana	Himalayan white pine
Quercus ilex	holly oak
Quercus virginiana	southern live oak
Sciadopitys verticillata	Japanese umbrella pine
Sequoia sempervirens	coast redwood
Tsuga canadensis	Canada hemlock

Sciadopitys verticillata, Japanese umbrella pine

Pinus thunbergiana, Japanese black pine

Large Focus Trees, Deciduous

LATIN	COMMON
Acer rubrum	scarlet maple
Fagus sylvatica	European beech
Ginkgo biloba	maidenhair tree
Jacaranda mimosifolia	green ebony
Liquidambar styraciflua	sweet gum
Liriodendron tulipfera	tulip tree
Pistacia chinensis	Chinese pistachio
Platanus	sycamore
Quercus acutissima	sawtooth oak
Robinia pseudoacacia	black locust
Zelkova serrata	sawleaf zelkova

PLANTS GROUPED BY USE

Betula platyphylla 'Japonica,' Japanese white birch

Medium-sized Trees, Deciduous

LATIN	COMMON
Albizia julibrissin	silk tree
Betula	birch
Carpinus	hornbeam
Celtis	hackberry
Cercidiphyllum japonicum	katsura tree
Gleditsia triacanthos	honey locust
Laburnum anagyroides	golden-chain tree
Morus alba	white mulberry
Nyssa sylvatica	sour gum
Populus tremuloides	quaking aspen
Punica granatum	pomegranate
Sophora japonica	Japanese pagoda tree
Sorbus aucuparia	European mountain ash
Styrax	snowbell
Tilia cordata	small-leaved linden

Medium-sized Border Trees, Evergreen

LATIN	COMMON
Acacia baileyana	golden mimosa
Callistemon viminalis	weeping bottlebrush
Cornus capitata	evergreen dogwood
Eriobotrya japonica	loquat
Ilex	holly
Magnolia	magnolia
Melaleuca linariifolia	flaxleaf paperbark
Prunus caroliniana	Carolina cherry laurel

Magnolia stellata, star magnolia

PLANTS GROUPED BY USE

Small Trees, Evergreen

LATIN	COMMON
Leptospermum laevigatum	Australian tea tree
Ligustrum lucidum	glossy privet
Nerium oleander	common oleander
Olea europaea	common olive
Osmanthus fragrans	sweet olive
Palmae	palms
Photinia fraseri	redtip photinia
Pyrus kawakamii	evergreen pear
Schinus terebinthifolius	Brazilian pepper tree

Prunus lusitanica, Portugal laurel

Syringa japonica, lilac

Small Trees, Deciduous

LATIN	COMMON
Acer buergeranum	trident maple
Acer davidii	David's maple
Acer ginnala	Amur maple
Acer griseum	paperbark maple
Acer palmatum	Japanese maple
Amelanchier	serviceberry
Bauhinia forficata	Brazilian butterfly tree
Cercis canadensis	redbud
Cladrastis lutea	yellowwood
Cornus florida	flowering dogwood
Cornus kousa	Kousa dogwood
Cotinus coggygria	smoke tree
Halesia carolina	wild olive
Lagerstroemia indica	crape myrtle
Malus floribunda	showy crab apple
Oxydendrum arboreum	sourwood
Parrotia persica	Persian parrotia
Prunus serrulata	Japanese flowering cherry
Prunus mume	Japanese apricot "plum"
Pyrus salicifolia 'Pendula'	weeping willow-leaved pear
Syringa japonica	Japanese tree lilac

PLANTS GROUPED BY USE

Prunus serrulata 'Pendula,' Japanese weeping cherry

Hedges, Evergreen

LATIN	COMMON	LATIN	COMMON
Abelia grandiflora	glossy abelia	*Nandina domestica*	heavenly bamboo
Bambusa	bamboo	*Osmanthus*	olive
Berberis	barberry	*Photinia*	photinia
Buxus	boxwood	*Pittosporum tobira*	Japanese pittosporum
Carissa	carissa	*Podocarpus*	podocarpus
Chamaecyparis leylandii	Leyland cypress	*Prunus mume*	flowering apricot "plum"
Chamaecyparis pisifera	Sawara cypress	*Prunus lusitanica*	Portugal laurel
Cotoneaster	cotoneaster	*Pyracantha*	fire thorn
Euonymus	spindle tree	*Raphiolepis*	raphiolepis
Juniperus	juniper	*Rosmarinus officinalis*	rosemary
Laurus nobilis	sweet bay	*Taxus*	yew
Leptospermum	tea tree	*Thuja*	arborvitae
Ligustrum	privet	*Viburnum*	viburnum
Myrtus communis	true myrtle		

PLANTS GROUPED BY USE

Hedges, Deciduous

LATIN	COMMON
Acer campestre	hedge maple
Berberis thunbergiana	Japanese barberry
Carpinus betulus	European hornbeam
Chaenomeles	flowering quince
Elaeagnus angustifolia	wild olive
Euonymus	spindle tree
Fagus sylvatica	European beech
Ligustrum	privet
Lonicera	honeysuckle
Rosa	rose
Weigela	weigela

Wisteria sinensis, Chinese wisteria

Euonymus alata, winged spindle tree

Vines, Hedges

LATIN	COMMON
Ampelopsis brevipedunculata	porcelain berry
Campsis	trumpet creeper
Clematis	virgin's bower
Hydrangea anomala	climbing hydrangea
Lonicera	honeysuckle
Schizophragma hydrangeoides	Japanese hydrangea vine
Wisteria sinensis	Chinese wisteria

PLANTS GROUPED BY USE

Hedera sp., upright ivy

Ground Covers

LATIN	COMMON
Arabis	rock cress
Arctostaphylos uva-ursi	common bearberry
Arenaria montana	sandwort
Carex	sedge
Chamaemelum nobile	chamomile
Chrysogonum virginianum	golden star
Duchesnea indica	Indian strawberry
Festuca	fescue
Fragaria chiloensis	beach strawberry
Galium odoratum	sweet woodruff
Gaultheria shallon	salal
Gelsemium sempervirens	Carolina jessamine
Glechoma hederacea	ground ivy
Hypericum	St.-John's-wort
Iberis sepervirens	edging candytuft
Juniperus	juniper

Vines, Evergreen

LATIN	COMMON
Bougainvillea	bougainvillea
Clematis armandii	evergreen clematis
Distictis	trumpet vine
Hedera	ivy
Jasminum	jasmine
Lonicera	honeysuckle
Passiflora	passionflower
Senecio confusus	Mexican flame vine
Stephanotis floribunda	Madagascar jasmine
Trachelospermum jasminoides	star jasmine

Juniperus davurica 'Aureovariegata,' **variegated juniper**

PLANTS GROUPED BY USE

LATIN	COMMON
Pachysandra terminalis	Japanese spurge
Parthenocissus quinquefolia	Virginia creeper
Sagina subulata	Irish moss, Scotch moss
Soleirilia soleirolii	baby's tears
Sollya heterophylla	Australian bluebell creeper
Stachys byzantina	lamb's ears
Taxus baccata 'Repandens'	spreading English yew
Teucrium chamaedrys	germander
Thymus	thyme
Trachelospermum	star jasmine
Veronica	speedwell
Vinca	periwinkle
Viola	violet

Acer palmatum 'Dissectum,' Japanese laceleaf maple

Pieris japonica, lily-of-the-valley bush

Compact Plants Around Rocks

LATIN	COMMON
Acer palmatum	Japanese maple
Berberis thunbergi	Japanese barberry
Betula pendula 'Trost's dwarf'	Trost's dwarf birch
Cedrus deodara	deodar cedar
Chaemcyparis obtusa	hinoki cypress
Cotoneaster	cotoneaster
Ilex crenata	dwarf Japanese holly
Picea	spruce
Pieris japonica	lily-of-the-valley bush
Pinus densiflora 'Umbraculifera'	tanyosho pine
Pinus mugo	mountian pine
Pinus strobus 'Nana'	dwarf white pine
Pinus sylvestris	dwarf Scotch pine
Tsuga canadensis	Canadian hemlock

PLANTS GROUPED BY USE

Pinus densiflora, Japanese red pine

Trees Next to a Pond or Stream

LATIN	COMMON
Acer rubrum	scarlet maple
Alnus	alder
Betula	birch
Fraxinus latifolia	Oregon ash
Laris laricina	American larch
Liquidambar styraciflua	American sweet gum
Quercus bicolor	swamp white oak
Quercus nigra	water oak
Salix	willow
Sequoia	coast redwood
Taxodium	swamp cypress

Shrubs Near Water

LATIN	COMMON
Andromeda polifolia	bog rosemary
Aronia arbutifolia	red chokeberry
Cornus stolonifera	red-twig dogwood
Gaultheria shallon	salal
Salix	willow
Sambucus canadensis	American elderberry
Vaccinium	vaccinium
Viburnum cassinoides	withe-rod

Salix babylonica, weeping willow

PLANTS GROUPED BY USE

Acer japonicum 'Aconitifolium,' full-moon maple

Trees Under a Canopy of Shade

LATIN	COMMON
Acer japonicum 'Aconitifolium'	full-moon maple
Acer palmatum	Japanese maple
Cercidiphyllum japonicum	katsura tree
Cercis canadensis	Eastern redbud
Davidia involucrata	dove tree
Laurus nobilis	sweet bay
Podocarpus	podocarpus
Stewartia	stewartia
Tree ferns	tree ferns

Shrubs in the Shade

LATIN	COMMON
Actaea	baneberry
Aucuba japonica	Japanese aucuba
Buxus	boxwood
Camellia	camellia
Daphne	daphne
Enkianthus campanulatus	enkianthus
Euonymus fortunei	spindel tree
Fatsia japonica	Japanese aralia
Fuchsia	fuchsia

PLANTS GROUPED BY USE

Acer japonicum 'Aconitifolium,' full-moon maple, close-up of leaves

LATIN	COMMON
Garenia jasminoides	gardenia
Hamamelis	witch hazel
Hydrangea	hydrangea
Nandina domestica	heavenly bamboo
Osmanthus	olive
Pieris	lily-of-the-valley bush
Rhododendron	azalea, rhododendron
Ribes sanguineum	pink winter currant
Skimmia japonica	skimmia
Symphoricarpos	snowberry
Taxus	yew
Vaccinium	vaccinium

Ornamental Grasses

LATIN	COMMON
Calamagrostis acutifolia 'Stricta'	feather reed grass
Carex	sedge
Coix lacryma-jobi	Job's tears
Cortaderia selloana	pampas grass
Deschampsia	hair grass
Hakonechloa macra 'Aureola'	Japanese forest grass
Imperata cylindrica 'Rubra'	Japanese blood grass
Milium effusum 'Aureum'	Bowles' golden grass
Molinia caerulea	purple moor grass
Panicum virgatum	switch grass
Pennisetum	fountain grass
Phalaris arundinacea	ribbon grass
Setaria palmifolia	palm grass
Stipa	feather grass

Nandina domestica, heavenly bamboo

Rhododendron 'Coral bells,' Kurume azalea

PLANTS GROUPED BY USE

For Interesting Bark

LATIN	COMMON
Acer davidii	David's maple
Acer griseum	paperbark maple
Acer palmatum 'Sango kaku'	coral bark maple
Betula	birch
Pinus bungeana	lacebark pine
Planaus	plane tree, sycamore
Populus alba	white poplar
Populus tremuloides	quaking aspen
Prunus serrulata	Japanese flowering cherry
Salix alba vitellina	white willow

Acer griseum, paperbark maple

Brilliant Fall Color

LATIN	COMMON
Acer	maple
Asimina triloba	pawpaw
Carpinus	hornbeam
Celtis	hackberry
Cercidiphyllum japonicum	katsura tree
Cladrastis lutea	yellow wood
Cornus	dogwood
Crataegus	hawthorn
Fagus	beech

Acer palmatum 'Omurayama,' Japanese maple

Acer palmatum 'Aoyagi,' yellow fall maple

PLANTS GROUPED BY USE

Acer palmatum 'Tana,' **Japanese maple**

LATIN	COMMON
Fraxinus	ash
Ginkgo biloba	maidenhair tree
Gleditsia triacanthos	honey locust
Koelreuteria bipinnata	Chinese flame tree
Lagerstroemia indica	crape myrtle
Latrix	larch
Liquidambar	sweet gum
Malus 'Prairiefire'	crab apple
Metasequoia glyptostroboides	dawn redwood
Morus	mulberry

LATIN	COMMON
Nyssa sylvatica	sour gum
Oxydendrum arboreum	sourwood
Pistacia chinensis	Chinese pistachio
Populus	poplar
Pseudolarix kaempferi	golden larch
Robinia	locust
Sapium sebiferum	Chinese tallow tree
Sassafras albidum	sassafras
Sorbus	mountain ash
Styrax japonicus	Japanese snowbell
Tilia	linden
Zelkova serrata	sawleaf zelkova

Acer palmatum 'Toyama nishiki,' **Japanese maple**

Acer palmatum 'Osakazuki,' **red maple**

SUGGESTED PLANT LIST

Latin	Common
Abies balsamea	balsam fir
Abies firma	Japanese fir
Abies homolepsis	nikko fir
Abies koreana	Korean fir
Abies lasiocarpa	alpine fir, Rocky Mountain fir
Abutilon hybridum	flowering maple, Chinese bellflower, Chinese lantern
Acer buergeranum	trident maple
Acer campestre	hedge maple
Acer circinatum	vine maple

Bambusa multiplex 'Riviereorum,' bamboo

Acer circinatum, vine maple

Latin	Common
Acer davidii	David's maple
Acer ginnala	Amur maple
Acer griseum	paperbark maple
Acer japonicum	full-moon maple
Acer palmatum	Japanese maple
Acer shirasawanum 'Aureum'	golden full-moon maple
Acorus gramineus	grassy-leaved sweet flag
Adiantum pedatum	five-finger fern, maidenhair fern
Agapanthus africanus	lily-of-the-Nile
Albizia julibrissin	silk tree
Alyssum wulfenianum	madwort
Andromeda polifolia	bog rosemary

SUGGESTED PLANT LIST

Latin	Common
Betula jacquemontii	birch
Betula maximowicziana	monarch birch
Betula papyrifera	canoe birch, paper birch
Betula pendula 'Trost's Dwarf'	European white birch
Betula platyphylla 'Japonica'	Japanese white birch
Bougainvillea	bougainvillea
Boxus microphylla 'Japonica'	Japanese boxwood
Broussonetia papyrifera	paper mulberry
Calocedrus decurrens	California incense cedar
Camellia japonica	common camellia
Carpinus betulus	European hornbeam

Boxus microphylla 'Japonica,' Japanese boxwood

Latin	Common
Androsace	rock jasmine
Anemone hybrida	Japanese anemone
Arbutus unedo	strawberry tree
Arctostaphylos uva-ursi	common bearberry
Ardisia japonica	marlberry
Artemisia stellerana	beach wormwood, Dusty-Miller
Athyrium	fern
Aucuba japonica	Japanese laurel
Bambusa	bamboo giant grasses
Berberis thunbergii	Japanese barberry

Calocedrus decurrens, incense cedar

SUGGESTED PLANT LIST

Latin	Common
Cedrus atlantica	Atlas cedar
Cedrus deodara	deodar cedar
Cedrus libani	cedar-of-Lebanon
Celtis sinensis	Chinese hackberry, Yunnan hackberry
Cercis canadensis	eastern redbud
Cercis chinensis	Chinese redbud
Chaenomeles	flowering quince
Chamaecyparis obtusa	hinoki cypress
Chamaecyparis pisifera	sawara cypress
Chionanthus retusus	Chinese fringe tree
Choisya ternata	Mexican orange
Cinnamoum camphora	camphor tree
Cladrastis lutea	yellowwood
Clematis	virgin's bower
Cornus kousa	kousa dogwood
Cornus mas	cornelian cherry
Cornus sanguinea	blood-twig dogwood

Chamaecyparis pisifera, **sawara cypress**

Chamaecyparis obtusa 'Hinoki nana,' **dwarf hinoki cypress**

SUGGESTED PLANT LIST

Chamaecyparis pisifera 'Filifera,' threadbranch cypress

Latin	Common
Corylus avellana 'Contorta'	European filbert, Harry Lauder's walking stick
Cotoneaster acutifolius	Peking cotoneaster
Cotoneaster apiculatus	cranberry cotoneaster
Cotoneaster microphyllus	rockspray cotoneaster
Crataegus pinnatifida	northeastern Asian hawthorn
Crocus	crocus
Cryptomeria japonica	Japanese cedar
Cycas revoluta	sago palm
Daphne odora	winter daphne
Dichondra micrantha	lawn dichondra
Elaegnus angustifolia	Russian olive
Erica	heath
Eriobotrya japonica	loquat
Euonymus alata	winged spindle tree
Euonymus americana	strawberry bush

Chamaecyparis obtusa 'Gracilis,' dwarf hinoki cypress

SUGGESTED PLANT LIST

Latin	Common
Euonymus japonica	spindle tree
Fagus crenata	Japanese beech
Fagus sylvatica 'Asplenifolia'	fernleaf beech
Fagus sylvatica 'Atropunicea'	copper beech, purple beech
Fagus sylvatica 'Laciniata'	cutleaf beech
Fagus sylvatica 'Purpurea pendula'	weeping copper beech
Fagus sylvatica 'Tricolor'	tricolor beech
Fatsia japonica	Japanese fatsia
Forsythia ovata	Korean golden-bells
Fraxinus ornus	flowering ash
Gardenia	gardenia
Gaultheria shallon	salal
Ginkgo biloba	maidenhair tree
Gleditsia triacanthos	honey locust
Hedera	ivy
Hydrangea anomala	climbing hydrangea
Hypericum calycinum	creeping St.-John's-wort
Ilex cornuta	Chinese holly
Ilex crenata	Japanese holly

Pinus densiflora 'Umbraculifera,' tanyosho pine

Juniperis procumebns 'Nana,' dwarf juniper

Latin	Common
Iris kaempferi	Japanese iris
Juniperus chinensis 'Procumbens'	Japanese garden juniper
Juniperus chinensis 'Procumbens nana'	green mound juniper
Juniperus chinensis sargentii	sargent juniper
Juniperus davurica expansa 'Aureovariegata'	variegated juniper
Juniperus horizontalis 'Wiltonii'	blue carpet juniper
Juniperus chinenesis 'Blaauw'	Blaauw's juniper, blue shimpaku
Juniperus virginiana 'Skyrocket'	columnar juniper

SUGGESTED PLANT LIST

Pinus mugo, mountain pine

Latin	Common
Metasequoia glyptostroboides	dawn redwood
Morus alba	white mulberry, silkworm mulberry
Nandina domestica	heavenly bamboo
Nelumbo	lotus
Nymphaea	water lily
Ophiopogon japonica	mondo grass
Parrotia persica	Persian parrotia
Penstemon	beard-tongue
Photinia fraseri	red-tip photinia
Photinia glabra	Japanese photinia
Picea abies 'Nidiformia'	nest spruce
Picea orientalis	Oriental spruce
Pieris japonica	lily-of-the-valley bush
Pieris taiwanensis	lily-of-the-valley bush snowdrift
Pinus bungeana	lacebark pine
Pinus densiflora	Japanese red pine
Pinus densiflora 'Umbraculifera'	tanyosho pine
Pinus mugo	mountian pine

Latin	Common
Juniperus rigida 'Pendula'	needle juniper
Lagerstroemia fauriei	Japanese crape myrtle
Larix kaempferi	Japanese larch
Liquidambar orientalis	Oriental sweet gum
Lonicera japonica	Japanese honeysuckle
Loropetalum chinense	Chinese razzleberry
Magnolia sieboldii	oyama magnolia
Magnolia stellata	star magnolia
Malus floribunda	Japanese flowering crab apple

Picea abies 'Nidiformis', nest spruce

SUGGESTED PLANT LIST

Latin	Common
Pinus parviflora	Japanese white pine
Pinus thunbergiana	Japanese black pine
Pistacia chinensis	Chinese pistachio
Pittosporum phillyraeoides	willow pittosporum
Primula japonica	Japanese primrose
Prunus avium	sweet cherry
Prunus lusitanica	Portugal laurel
Prunus sargentii 'Columnaris'	sargent cherry
Prunus serrula	Japanese flowering cherry
Prunus serrulata 'Pendula'	Japanese weeping cherry
Prunus serrulata 'Shirotae'	Mt. Fuji flowering cherry
Prunus serrulata 'Yae-shidare-higan'	double weeping cherry
Prunus mume	Japanese flowering apricot "plum"
Pseudolarix kaempferi/ Chrysolarix kaempferi	golden larch
Punica granatum	pomegranate
Pyracantha	fire thorn
Pyrus kawakamii	evergreen pear
Quercus myrsinifolia	Japanese live oak
Quercus suber	cork oak

Prunus sargentii 'Columnaris,' Japanese sargent cherry

Sciadopitys verticillata, Japanese umbrella pine

Latin	Common
Rhododendron/azalea	kurume hybrids, satsuki hybrids
Rhododendron japonicum	Japanese azalea
Rosmarinus officinalis	rosemary
Salix babylonica	weeping willow
Salix matsudana	Peking willow
Salix udensis 'Sekka'	Japanese fantail willow
Schizophragma hydrangeoides	Japanese hydrangea vine
Sciadopitys verticillata	Japanese umbrella pine

SUGGESTED PLANT LIST

Rhododendron 'Blue diamond,' azalea

Latin	Common
Viburnum davidii	David's viburnum
Viburnum plicatum 'Plicatum'	Japanese snowball
Wisteria floribunda	Japanese wisteria
Wisteria sinensis	Chinese wisteria
Zelkova serrata	sawleaf zelkova
Ziziphus jujuba	Chinese jujube
Zoysia tenuifolia	Korean velvet grass

Cedrus atlanticus 'Glauca pendula,' cedar

Latin	Common
Skimmia japonica	evergreen shrub
Styrax japonica	Japanese snowdrop tree, Japanese snowbell
Syringa reticulata	Japanese tree lilac
Taxus cuspidata	Japanese yew
Tilia cordata	little-leaf linden
Tsuga canadensis	Canadian hemlock
Ulmus parvifolia	Chinese elm, lacebark elm
Viburnum carlesii	Korean spice viburnum

Tsuga canadensis 'Cole's prostrate,' Canadian hemlock

INDEX